Advanced Praise for *Culturally Proficient Inquiry*

By Randall B. Lindsey, Stephanie M. Graham, R. Chris Westphal, Jr., and Cynthia L. Jew, Corwin Press (2007)

"What is best about this remarkable book is its constant reminder that the courage to do what is just and right for the 'underserved' comes to those who face the 'brutal facts,' listen to the difficult questions, and seek support and guidance from the educators in the field. This book is an inspiring companion needed now more than ever."

—**Sidney Morrison**,
Principal, Howard Wood Elementary School, Torrance, CA

"The authors take a comprehensive approach to educational reform, one that fosters schools' cultural proficiency in four broad areas: assessment and accountability, curriculum and instruction, home-school relations, and teacher professional development. They manage to both convey the magnitude and complexity of the problem of schools underserving their constituencies and illuminate a path to positive change."

—**Elise Trumball**,
Educational Researcher, California State University, Northridge

"The culturally proficient inquiry model provides us with a process for examining the strategies and practices that support or prevent equitable access to learning. Understanding what it means to be culturally proficient and becoming culturally proficient places of learning is fundamental to student success and achievement."

—**Sharon List**,
Superintendent, York Region District School Board, Ontario, Canada

"The authors effectively empower educators with the knowledge, will, and skill to close educational gaps. This book takes educators on a thorough journey of learning and reflection, examining data, presenting information, discussing best practices, and posing questions. It provides the tools, rubrics, and matrices to help educators review, revise, and measure their practices and progress toward cultural proficiency."

—Liebe Geft,
Director, Museum of Tolerance

"An outstanding field manual. It provides the context, framework, and tools for district and school staffs to have 'fierce conversations' about institutional and personal responsibility for closing the achievement gap. A must-read for those serious about educating all students."

—General Davie, Jr.,
Retired Superintendent, San Juan Unified School District, CA

"Finally, a publication that makes cultural proficiency understandable for school leaders and teaching staffs and provides the practical means for leaders to address cultural proficiency in schools, districts, and communities. A useful how-to guide for this critically important work."

—Joseph Condon,
Superintendent, Lawndale School District, CA

"A change in the rhetoric from underperforming stakeholders (be they students, parents, teachers, or staff) to underserved stakeholders is critically needed. Educators can change the rhetoric and shift the sense of responsibility onto the adults in the system who can do something about closing gaps and thereby educate others on how the deficit model of blaming those who are underperforming does nothing to transform the system to better serve all stakeholders."

—Beverly LeMay,
Director, Tools for Tolerance Programs, Museum of Tolerance

"The authors have created the ultimate practical resource for determining how to make cultural proficiency work in our organizations. A must-have for those of us who are seriously and genuinely committed to going on a journey toward cultural proficiency!"

—Tina Small,
Director of HRS Workforce and Organization Development,
Los Angeles County Office of Education

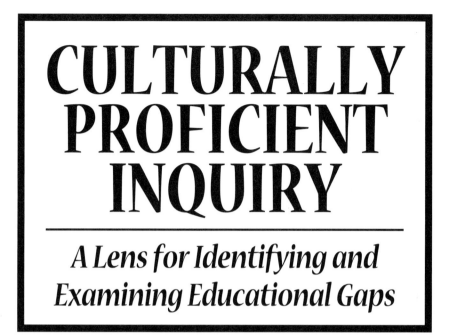

CULTURALLY PROFICIENT INQUIRY

A Lens for Identifying and Examining Educational Gaps

Randall B. Lindsey · Stephanie M. Graham

R. Chris Westphal, Jr. · Cynthia L. Jew

CORWIN PRESS

A SAGE Company

Thousand Oaks, CA 91320

For information:

Corwin Press
A SAGE Company
2455 Teller Road
Thousand Oaks, California 91320
www.corwinpress.com

SAGE India Pvt. Ltd.
B 1/I 1 Mohan Cooperative
   Industrial Area
Mathura Road, New Delhi 110 044
India

SAGE Ltd.
1 Oliver's Yard
55 City Road
London EC1Y 1SP
United Kingdom

SAGE Asia-Pacific Pte. Ltd.
33 Pekin Street #02–01
Far East Square
Singapore 048763

Printed in the United States of America.

Library of Congress Cataloging-in-Publication Data

Culturally proficient inquiry: a lens for identifying and examining educational gaps / Randall B. Lindsey, . . . [et al.].
    p. cm.
Includes bibliographical references and index.
ISBN 978-1-4129-2601-0 (cloth)
ISBN 978-1-4129-2602-7 (pbk.)
   1. Multicultural education—United States. 2. Education—Political asepects—United States. 3. Academic achievement—United States. I. Lindsey, Randall B. II. Title.

LC1099.3.C844 2008
370.11′5—dc22   2007036305

This book is printed on acid-free paper.

07   08   09   10   11   10 9 8 7 6 5 4 3 2 1

Acquisitions Editor:	Rachel Livsey
Managing Editor:	Dan Alpert
Editorial Assistants:	Phyllis Cappello, Tatiana Richards
Production Editor:	Eric Garner
Copy Editor:	Barbara Ray
Typesetter:	C&M Digitals (P) Ltd.
Proofreader:	Theresa Kay
Indexer:	Kathleen Paparchontis
Cover Designer:	Lisa Riley

Contents

Foreword

We are confronting an era in which multiple events are converging to bring America back to the reality from which it has been trying to escape. The nation is in denial about aspects of its history that hold the nation hostage. The claimed diversity of America is in many ways a façade reminiscent of Paul Laurence Dunbar's "We Wear the Mask" poem written a century ago. In the words of Dunbar, we are a nation wearing masks that "grin and lie." They "hide our cheeks and shade our eyes" (453). Our masks are an attempt to conceal centuries of a harsh history between us that has positioned people on different rungs of a social ladder and attempted to keep them there, largely on the basis of color. In spite of attempts to hide or run from our history, life repeatedly resurfaces it, giving us another chance to remove our masks, confront it, and be healed. Such is the case in public education today with the heightened attention to the so-called achievement gap. Life is once again giving the nation an opportunity to confront its history in order to confront the "achievement gap."

John Henrik Clark has reminded us of the power of history to shape the present.

> History isn't everything, but it is a starting point. History is a clock that people use to tell their political and cultural time of day. It is a compass they use to find themselves on the map of human geography. It tells them who they are, but more important, what they must do.

The emphasis the authors of *Cultural Proficient Inquiry* have placed on confronting our national history, as a way to address teaching and learning, presents an opportunity for personal and societal healing. It enables educators to confront the effects of history on their own constructs of self identity that in turn affect the manner in which they construct relationships with the children who enter their classrooms every day. Historians like Lerone Bennett,

Ron Takaki, and John Hope Franklin, with the assistance of modern science and technology, have "unmasked" the mythical renditions of history that rendered people of color invisible, portrayed them as savages, or reduced them to child-like caricatures of themselves. They have confronted the manufactured portrayals of White conquerors and enslavers as flawless heroes who created the culture and wealth of America by their own genius, unaided by the genius of involuntary African immigrants brought to these shores as slaves or the indigenous people Europeans found here upon their arrival.

Although the uncovered history is revealing the vital role African Americans and the indigenous people of the continent played in the making of America, the effects of this mythical history are not so easily erased. They have shaped the American psyche that, in turn, has shaped the "hidden curriculum" (Bennett) of schooling. The images carefully constructed to keep people of color subjugated remain deeply embedded in the minds of the nation's people, serving as powerful tools for maintaining a permanent underclass and a permanent class of privilege. The nation's schools are major purveyors of those images.

The influence of America's history plays out in classrooms across this nation every day. Despite efforts to eradicate the cultures of a people that predate colonialism, the influence of history on the formation of cultures among the descendants of Africa and the ancient American continent still abides in the children of this generation— passed down from one generation to the next. Cultures carved by a people determined to live and love and create in spite of their oppression in America are also in the children who show up at school every year expecting to learn. Their intellect, their cognitive structures, their ways of being, their very *Being* have been molded in the crucibles of their lives shared with families and communities where their learning first took place. This is the intellectual, linguistic, and cultural capital they present to their teachers for learning. "Every function in the cultural development of the child appears on the stage twice, on two planes. First on the social plane, and then on the psychological; first between people, and then inside the child" (Vygotsky, 1978, p. 57).

But this is precisely the capital that mainstream white Americans have rejected and demeaned to maintain their positions on the "map of human geography" (Clarke). Inevitably, teachers and students who are products of their histories and cultures bring their identities to the place called school where a daily confrontation takes place. The culture of the classroom is the culture of dominance created in the crucible of our American history, and all other cultures are barred from entrance. This is the fundamental issue behind the achievement gap.

It will not be solved with more and more remediation, followed by more testing and more policies and laws. A confrontation with our history and its effects on the human interaction in our schools bears the seeds for the nation's redemption and an end to the achievement gap, which is only a symptom of a much deeper problem.

Paulo Freire, among others, established the principle that teaching is an act of liberation that cannot be achieved by attempting to deposit knowledge into children's heads in the way we bank money. This understanding is fundamental to the concept of cultural proficiency. Sufficient cognitive research has led to understandings that learning occurs when the teacher skillfully taps into students' prior knowledge through the cognitive structures the child's past experiences have created. A deeply rooted disrespect for the cultures of African American, Native American, and Latino peoples created by our American history frequently prevents teachers from applying this principle when teaching the children of these cultures. The "hidden curriculum" (Bennett) of our schools is based in assumptions of the superiority of mainstream American culture and inferiority of any other cultures (p. 183). Therefore, whether consciously or unconsciously, teachers set about ridding students of language, behaviors, and cognitive structures that are not consistent with the culture presumed to be superior, in the name of meeting these children's needs. In the process students whose cultures differ from mainstream American culture are robbed of the intellectual capital every child derives from her or his culture, providing the basis for future learning. We cannot expect to close an achievement gap by violating the basic principles of teaching and learning. The so-called achievement gap will never be closed while schools deny some children the conditions for intellectual engagement and grant free access to others, based on skin color and social position.

Failure to confront this fundamental violation of teaching and learning explains why the pursuit of equity in education continues to elude our nation. America is a nation caught on the horns of its own dilemma. On the one hand America would like to be perceived as living up to the principles of liberty and justice espoused in its founding documents. On the other hand, the nation is unwilling to confront the barriers to access designed to keep people of color apart and subservient. Our schools remain the "ideal" place to replicate the relationships of our past. The conditions of the twenty-first century say to the nation it can no longer afford to replicate the past. In a century when the so-called minority will become the majority, the nation's well-being is severely threatened by a majority population that is both poor and uneducated.

Education, which is a powerful force for reforming a society, has an opportunity to break from a history of inequities if the people who teach our children are willing to confront their own identities and cultural orientations shaped by their place in American history. In the process, they will consent to their own liberation in order to liberate their students.

The authors of this book have persisted for decades in awakening the soul of teaching by creating an awareness and useful tools to promote cultural proficiency. This newest book identifies the powerful link between the nation's history and the nation's present crisis in public education. It offers opportunities for adults to understand and embrace cultural proficiency.

The teacher role described in the following passage by Vygotsky again provides insight about the teachers children need. It helps us all know what cultural proficiency will look like when we find it.

> *"The teacher's work is particularly complex because in the first place, the teacher must be well oriented to the regularities of the child's personal activity, that is, know the child's psychology; in the second place, the teacher must know the particular social dynamics of the child's social setting and in the third place, the teacher must know about the possibilities of his or her own pedagogical activity to use these sensibly and thus raise to a new level the activity, consciousness, and personality of his or her charges" (1995, p. 17).*

—Sylvia Rousseau

References

Bennett, Christine (2001, Summer). Genres of research in multicultural education. *Educational Research, 71* (2), 171–217.

Bennett, Lerone, Jr. (2003). *Before the* Mayflower: *A history of Black America* (5th ed.). Chicago, Illinois: Johnson.

Dunbar, Paul Laurence (1993). English and American—The collected poetry of Paul Laurence Dunbar. (J. M. Braxton, Ed.) *Choice. Middletown, 31* (3), 453.

Franklin, John Hope, & Moss, Alfred A., Jr. (1988). *From slavery to Freedom: A history of Negro Americans* (6th ed.). New York, New York: Knopf.

Freire, Paolo (1970). *Pedagogy of the oppressed.* (M. B. Ramos, Trans.) New York, New York: Herder and Herder.

Takaki, Ronald (1993). *A different mirror: A history of multicultural America.* Boston: Little, Brown and Company.

Vygotsky, Lev (1978). *Mind in society: The development of higher psychological processes.* (V. J.-S. Michael Cole, Ed.) Cambridge, Massachusetts: Harvard University Press.

Vygotsky, Lev (1995, April). The influence of L.S. Vygotsky on education theory, research, and practice. (V. V. Davydov, Ed.) *Educational Researcher, 24,* 12–24.

Preface

Cultural Proficiency as a Paradigm for Democracy

Cultural proficiency serves as a mindset for educators who are dedicated to effective cross-cultural practices. When conceptualizing and constructing this book, we called on the work of many other authors who share our passion for making our democracy more inclusive and who see our public schools as central to that process. The work of Terry Cross and Michael Fullan epitomizes for us the intersections of moral centeredness and commitment to democratic outcomes for all citizens.

Cross and his colleagues (1989) developed the initial concepts of cultural competence and cultural proficiency. The standards of cultural competence provide the framework for the rubrics presented herein; they are "a set of congruent behaviors, attitudes, and policies that come together in a system, agency, or amongst professionals and enables that system, agency, or those professionals to work effectively in cross-cultural situations" (p. iv).

Fullan (2003) provides criteria for the moral purpose of our work as educators being "that all students and teachers benefit in terms of desirable goals, that the gap between high and low performers becomes less as the bar is raised, that ever-deeper goals are pursued, and that the culture of the school becomes so transformed that continuous improvement relative to the previous three components becomes built in" (p. 31).

Authors' Invitation

Welcome to this, the fifth book authored by one or more of the authors of the original *Cultural Proficiency: A Manual for School Leaders* by Randall B. Lindsey, Kikanza Nuri Robins, and Raymond D. Terrell.

With this book, Randy has teamed with three colleagues who have developed and are nurturing culturally proficient practices in educational institutions:

- Stephanie M. Graham works regionally and nationally from the Los Angeles County Office of Education to establish culturally proficient, equitable practices in local schools.
- R. Chris Westphal, Jr., established effective assessment practices within the San Juan (California) Unified School District and, in retirement, has a practice serving other school districts.
- Cynthia L. Jew has developed and administers leadership and counseling programs at California Lutheran University employing culturally proficient practices in service of degree and certification candidates.

Almost three years ago, the four of us met to discuss what it would take to foster discussions and provoke actions leading to ever-higher levels of achievement and closing important educational gaps for historically underserved students. Three of us were in the midst of a three-year professional development involvement with the San Juan Unified School District to bring a cultural proficiency lens to educators' discussions of how best to use assessment data in developing practices to meet the educational needs of students. Two of us were developing a new Educational Doctorate program at California Lutheran University and were working with faculty colleagues on strategies for making an applied doctoral program responsive to local school needs. From those discussions emerged the framework for this book.

The initial emphasis was on developing the rubrics presented in Chapter 6. Development of the rubrics became the "boots on the ground" link that many educators needed in order to make cultural proficiency concrete and applied. Although we were, and remain, resistant to developing "how-to strategies," we understood the value in developing models of practice. In the last year, each of us has had the opportunity to work with educators in varied settings to test the utility of the rubrics. Reactions ranged from those who were grateful for illustrations and who began to develop their own rubrics to those who experienced dissonance in having some of their current practices situated at the "destructiveness," "incapacity," or "blindness" points on the continuum.

The Task That Lies Before Us

Since 2001, school districts throughout the United States have been mandated to "leave no child behind" (No Child Left Behind Act [NCLB], 2001). Although several states had implemented similar programs prior to 2001, NCLB has drawn concerted national attention to the disparities of achievement among demographic groups. Throughout the country, many school districts receiving federal funds for educating students of poverty (e.g., Title I) have used this mandate as an opportunity to examine student achievement data in ways that clearly identify the achievement gaps that exist between students who have been historically well served by our schools and those who have been marginalized in many ways.

Furthermore, recent data from the National Association of Educational Progress (NAEP) indicate that districts across the country are using assessment data to inform decisions about curriculum, instruction, and learning outcomes and are making headway in narrowing the gap (Edwards, 2006; Perie, Moran, & Lutkus, 2005). Other districts struggle in closing the gap because educators often blame students for their family and social circumstances. These educators hold beliefs based on negative racial, social, and cultural stereotypes about who learns and at what levels students can achieve. Fullan (1993, 1999, 2003) repeatedly emphasizes that reduction of the achievement gap is the moral responsibility of all educators and that we must move beyond ourselves to appropriately serve all sectors of our communities.

It is important to understand that generations of well-intentioned adult stakeholders have attempted to make education accessible and ensure academic success for students who were at risk of falling between the educational and social cracks, but despite the best intentions, have fallen woefully short of their goals. It is now an irony that the very students who have been ignored or left behind by our P–12 educational system now depend on the adult communities of teachers, counselors, administrators, and parents or guardians to create environments and conditions for their academic success.

This book guides readers from a macroperspective of struggles to make the democracy in this country inclusive and to develop local capacity for ensuring educational access, equity, and high achievement for everybody's children. We hope that by understanding the past and the present, we can better prepare ourselves for the work in front of us. However, this book goes beyond helping readers understand the past and the enormity of the task before us.

This book culminates with three major activities:

- collecting and examining data about your students,
- having conversations with your colleagues about the collected data, and
- making decisions about your practice that provide your students with equitable access to learning.

These three steps invite you to examine your school, to collect pertinent qualitative and quantitative data, to use cultural proficiency to frame your professional conversations and take steps to begin to close gaps that matter for children who matter. In Part I, we present the historical context and rationale that inform the need for culturally proficient practices. In Part II, we present the opportunity to gather and analyze data about your school. In Part III, we introduce you to the ABC Case Study School to examine their processes and protocols to guide your own.

According to Perie et al. (2005), the current achievement gap data reflect the need for inclusive discussions that enable educators to play a key role in the intentional unfolding of the democracy in such a way that students who graduate from our P–12 schools

- are able to function at high academic levels,
- are able to function well in our increasingly diverse society, and
- have a positive and palpable sense of their own and others' cultures.

As you envision these goals, you may want to invite even more stakeholders into your inquiry process to share responsibility for the work, encouragement along the journey, and ownership of the results.

Randall B. Lindsey, Escondido, California

Stephanie M. Graham, Los Angeles, California

R. Chris Westphal, Jr., Cameron Park, California

Cynthia L. Jew, Castaic, California

Acknowledgments

Randy, Stephanie, Chris, and Cindy honor the valiant educational leaders at all levels of the system who work tirelessly to make our dream for culturally proficient classrooms and schools a reality. We are deeply grateful for the support, encouragement, and patience of family, friends, and colleagues who encouraged us at every stage in the development of this book. We are especially appreciative of each other for the commitment of time, resources, and energy it took to write this book.

Heartfelt appreciation goes to Rachel Livsey for her support, not only for our work but also for the work of all authors involved with democratic, equity-based education. Similarly, thank you many times to Phyllis Cappello, who keeps us on task and timeline and does so in a supportive manner.

This book would not have the conceptual framework of cultural proficiency without the work of Terry Cross, Kikanza Nuri Robins, Raymond D. Terrell, Delores B. Lindsey, Laraine Roberts, Franklin CampbellJones, and Richard Martinez. This book was informed and shaped by their previous work on cultural competence and cultural proficiency.

If cultural proficiency is the moral heart of this book, the rubrics are the hands and eyes for doing this work. Several experts served to validate the content of the rubrics, and our appreciation for their work goes to Brenda CampbellJones, Franklin CampbellJones, Richard Gregory, Delores B. Lindsey, Kikanza Nuri Robins, and Raymond D. Terrell for the many hours they devoted to parsing every word, concept, and nuance in the 140 cells that make up the rubrics.

Delores B. Lindsey and Henri Mondschein are deeply appreciated for their contributions to this book. Delores contributed many hours of feedback on each stage of the final manuscript. Her knowledge of the subject, skills with editorial feedback, and passion for this work contributed immeasurably to our final product. We also thank Henri Mondschein from California Lutheran University, who assisted with the research and editing for this book. Henri provided detailed research for the historical details that proved to be elusive, but not beyond his considerable skills!

The contributions of the following reviewers are greatly acknowledged:

Beverly Edman
Middle School Principal
Golden, CO

Dr. Steve Jenkins
Professor
University of Texas

Dr. Linda Jungwirth
Coordinator, Center for the Advancement of Small
   Learning Environments
Redlands, CA

John Krownapple
Professional Development Facilitator
Ellicot City, MD

About the Authors

Randall B. Lindsey, PhD, is Emeritus Professor, California State University, Los Angeles. He is coauthor of four books and a video on cultural proficiency. Randy is a former high school teacher, school administrator, and staff developer on issues of school desegregation and equity. He consults and coaches school districts and universities as they develop culturally proficient practices. Randy is enjoying this phase of life as a grandparent, as an educator, and in support of just causes (randallblindsey@aol.com).

Stephanie M. Graham, MA, is an educational consultant in Los Angeles. Her work centers on issues of diversity, educational equity, and closing educational gaps for underserved students and families. Stephanie is a former high school teacher, administrator, and college professor. She consults with school districts and agencies to develop culturally proficient practices leading to equitable outcomes for students, staff, customers, and clients (culturalcompetence.stephanie@gmail .com).

R. Chris Westphal, Jr., EdD, is an educational consultant with 30 years of experience as a director of research and evaluation, director of special education, and director of pupil personnel services. He has focused on cultural equity issues as a researcher and is a cultural proficiency coach and trainer for school districts. Chris enjoys his family, friends, photography, and the outdoors, and is an avid sports fan (westphal.chris@gmail.com).

Cynthia L. Jew, PhD, is Professor and Chair of the Educational Psychology department at California Lutheran University. In addition to her work in resiliency, she consults and collaborates with parents of special-needs children. As a psychologist, she is dedicated to systemic interventions that reflect culturally proficient best practices. Cindy's family has been blessed with two adopted children from China, one of whom is profoundly deaf and wears bilateral cochlear implants (cjew@clunet.edu).

I dedicate this book to Delores for being who she is in our world.

—Randy

I dedicate this book to my family for their lessons about social justice and to Randy, Angie, and Darline for believing that I could teach it to others.

—Stephanie

I dedicate this book to my girls, who continually inspire me.

—Chris

I dedicate this book to our children, Kiera and Jordyn, whose lives exemplify courage, faith, and love.

—Cindy

Part I
Creating Culturally Proficient Schools

Culturally Proficient Inquiry Is Based on the Will to Educate Our Students

W e have written this book to provide you with a way to gather and analyze data about demographic groups of students in your school and to make decisions that affect

- the academic achievement patterns of students,
- the cocurricular and access experiences of students, and
- the manner in which educators describe and discuss demographic groups of students identified as under performing.

The book is designed to provide you with the skills and knowledge to engage in professional conversations so that you may serve the academic and cocurricular needs of all demographic groups of students in your school. We have constructed this book in such a way that each of the three parts adds to knowledge and skills for closing the achievement gap. The chapters that comprise the three parts of the book serve as building blocks for your knowledge and skill development:

- Part I provides an historical perspective for achievement gap issues;
- Part II develops a context for the value, importance and limitations of data; and
- Part III guides you in constructing a profile of your school that conforms to the graphic organizer in Figure III.1.

Figure I.1 on the following page represents a graphic organizer for Part I of this book. In the subsequent introductions, Parts II and III, the graphic organizer is expanded upon and represented as Figures II.1 and III.1. The three corners of the triangle represent data you will be collecting to address equity issues in your school:

- Data set #1, student achievement, is presented in Chapter 7,
- Data set #2, student access data, is presented in Chapters 8 and 9, and
- Data set #3, profiles of educator conversations about students identified as under performing, are presented in Chapter 10.

As you proceed to the introductions to Parts II and III, the graphic organizers add layers of information for you to study and integrate into your work. Most important, you will have tools for you and your professional learning community to use in responding to the academic and cocurricular needs of your students.

Part I comprises two chapters constructed for you to read and reflect on as you consider your work in schools serving students from diverse cultural backgrounds. We assume that you have an abiding interest in education (i.e., aide, teacher, counselor, administrator, parent and/or interested member of the community) and are seeking to sharpen your knowledge and skills as you work with fellow educators to provide a high-level education to all children and youth. Our definition of *high-level* education transcends the current focus on often-narrow, research-tested methods to the more general education afforded all children and youth. When we speak of the *achievement gap,* we examine the academic performance of demographic groups of students. But we do not stop there. We also speak to the achievement gap of children and youth who are locked in insulated school systems that provide them with a sanitized curriculum that shelters them from learning about the rich history, literature, art, and music of people who are culturally different from them.

The advent of national and state-level school reforms have thrust the issue of achievement gaps onto the public stage as if it were a new topic. Chapter 1 provides a brief historical overview of equity gaps that have been institutionalized from the inception of our country. The struggle to provide equal or equitable access to voting and educational opportunities continues to be part of the drama of the unfolding democracy in the United States. Cultural Proficiency is borne out of the desire of educators wanting to ensure that our educational practices are designed and implemented to best serve all demographic groups of students. We believe this chapter provides you, the reader, with an historical context for the decisions and actions you take.

Chapter 2 reviews the four tools of Cultural Proficiency—the Guiding Principles of Cultural Proficiency, the Cultural Proficiency Continuum, the Five Essential Elements of Cultural Competence, and the Barriers to Cultural Proficiency. We recommend that you and your colleagues take considerable time to read, study, and discuss these tools as they are foundational to using the rubrics presented in Chapter 5. The rubrics are metrics by which you can gauge the extent to which adult conversation at your school assumes responsibility for all students achieving at high levels.

Each chapter opens with a *Getting Centered* section followed by spaces for you to record your responses. Your written responses serve as a journal for your equity self-study learning journey. The chapters also include opportunities for *Reflection* by providing questions to deepen your thinking about your practice and your learning.

Take your time. Read, reflect, write, and read some more. This is your learning journey.

Figure I.1   Culturally Proficient Inquiry

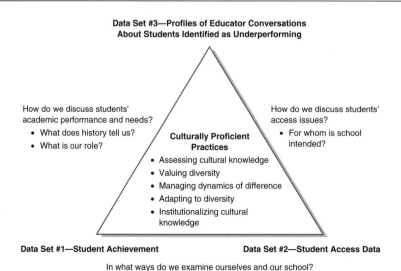

1

The Unfolding of the Democracy as a Moral Imperative

. . . a high-quality public school system is essential, not only for parents who send their children to these schools but also for the public good as a whole.

—Fullan (2003, p. 4)

Getting Centered

Who are you? To what cultural groups do you belong? How might you describe the cultures of your students? How do they identify culturally? How might the perceived gap between your cultural identities and the cultural identities of your students affect your ability to educate? How might the perceived gap affect your students' ability to learn? What are some of the reasons you are interested in reading this book? We invite you to write your responses to these questions in the space below:

_____

_____

_____

_____

The *Why* of Our Approach

The questions in the "Getting Centered" activity above might provoke some interesting reactions in you. You may not have thought about the gap between your cultural identity and the cultural identities of your students. Or, you may have thought deeply about these questions and are disturbed that many of your colleagues remain seemingly unaware of what is so obvious to you. Whatever your responses, they are right for you at this time.

As you read, think about, and discuss the information in this chapter, you will gain important background information to inform your professional conversations and help you develop a rationale for closing the achievement gap that transcends current reform mandates. Think about the "Getting Centered" questions and the various responses of fellow participants. Rather than agreeing or disagreeing with perspectives shared by colleagues, allow and encourage multiple perspectives to inform your professional conversations and use them as important keys to better know about the academic and social needs of all demographic groups of students in your school.

In this chapter, we present a comprehensive context for considering equity issues in your school. Specifically, this chapter provides

- a context for the past, with an historical overview for equity and equality in the United States;
- a context for the present, with a review of current factors that contribute to learning and achievement gaps as they manifest in today's schools;
- a review of common themes and best practices that correlate with closing learning, access, and achievement gaps; and
- an exhortation for taking personal and collective responsibility for closing gaps that matter for our children who matter.

Context for the Past: A Brief Historical Overview of Equity and Equality in Voting and Education in the United States

Two benefits of our democratic form of government are the right to vote and access to a free public education. Yet, access to voting and education came about by struggles throughout the country and in an uneven fashion. Universal basic rights of voting and education were conferred first on white males, then white women, and then people of color.

When the formal U.S. government was created in 1789, the only people who had the right to vote were property-owning white men (Hudson, 1999; Kousser, 1984). Large segments of the population—African slaves and freedmen, People of the First Nations,[1] women, and non-property-owning white men—were not provided this most basic of democratic rights. The men who created the democracy put into place a governmental system that was not fully democratic and denied to many groups full access to the universal promises set forth in the Declaration of Independence and the U.S. Constitution, the documents that were created to ensure democracy. Ironically, the very people initially excluded from the basic rights of citizenry used the judicial, legislative, and executive tools provided in the U.S. Constitution to gain the right to vote as well as other fundamental rights such as property ownership, access to public education, and service in the military.

Not until the middle of the 19th century was the right to vote extended to white males universally, and early in the 20th century to white women. Similarly, in the first half of the 19th century formal education was almost universally limited to those who could afford to attend private or parochial schools, resulting in a disproportionate number of white males being educated. An egregious example of education being systematically denied to large segments of the population was the prohibition in many states against allowing African slaves to learn to read (Douglass, 1845/1960). This country's legacy of denying education and educational access for some groups was so entrenched that not until some 80 years after the founding of this country did Horace Mann, the first Secretary for the Board of Education in Massachusetts, argue for a free public education for every child, an act that led to our nation's first compulsory education law (Richardson, 1980).

---

1. We are using People of the First Nations as a term of choice for indigenous native people who trace their roots to the period before the arrival of Europeans.

Compulsory education laws in the United States benefited European immigrants from Ireland, Germany, Italy, and Eastern European countries during the mid-19th to the early 20th century. Although these immigrant groups each entered U.S. society near the bottom rung of the social-class ladder, within two to three generations they were well represented in the burgeoning middle class. Still, as exploited as many of these immigrants were, they entered the United States with rights and privileges not afforded to People of the First Nations or to early African Americans (Takaki, 1993). These events demonstrate that the educational playing field has never been level for some groups and help to explain the deeply seated roots of inequality in U.S. education.

Technically, African Americans and other people of color were granted basic rights of voting and education with the 13th, 14th, and 15th Amendments to the U.S. Constitution in the late 1860s, but it took the 1964 and 1965 Civil Rights Acts to make those rights authentic and functional (Franklin & Moss, 1988; Sigler, 1998). That President George W. Bush signed an extension of the 1965 Voting Rights Act into law on July 26, 2006, is ongoing proof of inequities that continue to abide in our country and are too often reflected in our schools.

At the beginning of the twentieth century, few of what we now call school-age populations were attending school beyond sixth grade (Richardson, 1980; Unger, 2001). The expansion of industry in the first half of the 20th century and the technological explosion that followed World War II set the stage for the comprehensive school system that we have today. It is often a surprise to many that mandatory universal education through Grade 12 is a very modern occurrence. As of 2002, twenty-seven states have compulsory education requirements only to the attainment of age 16 (National Center for Education Statistics, 2005). For this nation's poor, the economic incentives of choosing work over higher education reinforce undereducation that leads to underemployment, undercompensation, and chronic, often irreversible, underclass social and economic status. This spiraling effect of who was educated in our schools—public, private, independent, or parochial—has laid the foundation for many of the inequities now evident in our schools.

Struggles for equality continued into the latter half of the 20th century. Mexican Americans, African Americans, Asian Americans, First Nations people, poor Americans, women, and children have had to resort to legal processes to gain access to the same education afforded middle-class white males. Legal processes such as *Mendez vs. Westminster* (1947), *Brown vs. Topeka Board of Education* (1954,

1955), the 1964 Civil Rights Act, *Lau vs. Nichols* (1974), *Williams vs. State of California* (2004), and Title IX Education Amendments (1972) are representative of the extent to which nondominant groups have had to struggle to have access to equitable educational opportunities. And the sad corollary to legal challenges for educational equality in the last half of the 20th century is that the education community initiated none of the legislative or judicial reviews to remedy these inequities in access to education. In reality, we in the educational establishment have been complicit in maintaining systems and practices that limit educational access and outcomes for nondominant groups in our society.

■ Reflection

What is your reaction to the points raised in this historical overview? In what ways, if any, does this section inform your understanding of current educational gaps in your school? Of economic and societal gaps in this country?

_____

_____

_____

_____

Context for the Present: Factors That Contribute to Learning and Achievement Gaps in Today's Schools

■ The Achievement Gap—1970 to the Present

Today most educators are aware of the phenomenon known as the *achievement gap* but may not know for certain how it manifests, whether we are making progress narrowing it, or exactly which groups of students are affected most by it. During the period from the 1970s to the 1990s, progress was made in closing the achievement gap (Grissmer & Flanagan, 2001). Haycock (2001) reported that the achievement gap between African American and white students from the 1970s to the 1990s was cut in half, and the gap separating Latino and white students declined by one-third. That progress came to a halt, however, and during the period from 1990 to 2004, African American 17-year-old students demonstrated a drop in achievement scores on the National Assessment of Educational Progress (NAEP) in reading and mathematics. Since that time, the gaps have widened again between white and Asian American students and their African American, Latino, and First Nations counterparts.

■ What We Know About the Academic Achievement Gap

In order to study the achievement gap, it is important to know what it is and is not, and which student groups are affected the most by it. The achievement gap is not about random results that vary from year to year for random student groups. The achievement gap in this context describes patterns of performance over time between white and Asian American middle-class students and their African American, Latino, and First Nations counterparts. Because students of poverty are disproportionately represented in these three racial-ethnic groups, we cannot overlook poverty as an intersecting variable to understand the achievement gap, but race and ethnicity are the more salient variables, with disturbingly entrenched patterns apparent for students of color. As difficult as it is to accept, the achievement gap has a face, and it is more about racial-ethnic demographic disparities than it is about economic differences.

The disturbing fact is that the achievement gap in this country correlates significantly with student racial-ethnic group membership. We have to face the brutal facts of these cultural correlates if we are to get serious about narrowing and closing the educational gaps that matter. We must examine what it is that affects our ability or inability to provide quality education to certain student groups. The first important fact to understand about the achievement gap is that it is demographic (Perie, Moran, & Lutkus, 2005; Peske & Haycock, 2006).

What other brutal facts must we confront if we hope to narrow and close these gaps for our students? Other facts that we know about the achievement gap but may prefer not to know or choose to ignore are these:

- The achievement gap is historical. Documentation of the academic achievement gap is well chronicled, at least back to the 1960s (Jencks & Phillips, 1999; Perie et al., 2005; Rothstein, 2004).

- The achievement gap is quantifiable. Gaps between student demographic groups can be noted in the following areas, just to name a few:
  o grade distributions and test scores,
  o course placement and selection,
  o grade promotion and graduation,
  o college entrance and completion, and
  o disciplinary referrals and consequences (Bay Area School Reform Collaborative, 2001; Harvard Civil Rights and Advancement Project, 2000; Johnston & Viadero, 2000).
- The disparity between student demographic groups is also evident from qualitative data about the following:
  o lowered beliefs and expectations,
  o inadequate resource allocation,
  o exclusion of students' backgrounds in curriculum materials,
  o underqualified, underprepared teachers,
  o strained teacher/student/family relationships,
  o inadequate and unsafe buildings and facilities, and
  o compromised wellness and poor health that affect students' ability to attend school regularly, arrive on time, and be ready to learn (Bay Area School Reform Collaborative, 2001; Johnston & Viadero, 2000).
- The achievement gap persists in urban, suburban, and rural schools (Lee, 2002).
- The achievement gap is not just about test scores. It correlates also with gaps in wellness, school readiness, opportunities to learn, opportunities to access educational programs and support, grade promotion and graduation, post-school opportunities including college entrance, employment and employability, and earnings (Berliner, 2005).

The data are extant, and the conclusions are clear. The achievement gap has a face—it is the faces of our African American, Latino, First Nations, and poor students. We can recognize the achievement gap by all of the above ways that it manifests. We cannot confront it, however, unless we are able to see it, describe it, and talk about it accurately and honestly with the blindfolds off.

Johnston and Viadero's (2000) series on the achievement gap cited a surprising lack of knowledge about the topic by educators, especially since it had been well documented since at least the 1960s. The current context of public school accountability with its focus on test scores, high-stakes tests, and school ranking has made the achievement gap among demographic groups a public issue. However, other mitigating factors associated with the gap often prove challenging for educators to discuss let alone to confront successfully, leaving important issues ignored because of their complexity and sensitivity. Confounding our ability to make progress in closing gaps are mandates to include English learners' and special needs students' test scores in school accountability reports, lack of qualified teachers and teacher training, inadequate funding and other resources, and high turnover of teachers and administrators in schools with the greatest need for stability.

Although some of these factors are predicaments that we need to learn to cope with, others are problems that we can begin to address to stem widening gaps in schools. The first steps we can take are to remove the blinders, to stop blaming underserved communities for their lack of progress, and to understand the conditions that are barriers to the education of many of our children. Perhaps by understanding, we can demystify the complexity of the gaps and begin to take steps to narrow and close them.

■ Reflection

How has the information in this section of the chapter deepened your understanding of the achievement gap? What new information did you learn? How will you use this information to close gaps in your own school?

_____

_____

_____

_____

■ Current Factors Contributing to the Achievement Gap

Johnston and Viadero (2000) and McREL (2000), in their investigations of the achievement gap, offer no single explanation for its existence, but describe several factors that are among the most widely researched and accepted to explain the current learning and achievement gap for African American, Latino, and First Nations children. Whereas some are beyond our direct control as educators, most are within our sphere of direct influence. The following section identifies factors that contribute to educational gaps for children. As you review them, reflect on which issues are within your control and how you might begin to mitigate the effects of these conditions on underperforming students.

Ineffective, Disengaging Instruction

Themes that emerge about classrooms in low-performing schools indicate nonrigorous coursework, ineffective instruction, and disengaging classroom discourse. McREL's (2000) review of studies on the achievement gap consistently cites disproportionately more African American and Latino students than white students taking nonchallenging academic coursework and curriculum. McREL (2000) further reports that immigrant children are even more limited by being placed in rigid tracking and separate curricular paths with no opportunity to take college-track courses, but as a substitute "receive outdated, ineffective vocational training that will do them little good on the job" (p. 2).

Learning for Latino and African American students is further compromised when teachers fail to differentiate instruction for learning style, readiness, interest, experiences, and students' language and linguistic styles, or when teachers do not take the time to get to know their students in order to connect learning experiences to students' backgrounds. When teachers do not know about their students or their cultures, they often fail to engage them in class discussions, wrongly construing their learning patterns or deference to authority as lack of interest or academic ability. Disengaged students do not learn at the same rate as students who are more actively participating in classroom activities (Educational Research Service, 2003; McREL, 2000).

Underqualified Teachers

The Education Trust (Haycock, 2001) reports compelling evidence that students in schools with high concentrations of students of color and poor students are more likely to be taught by underqualified teachers, a condition with far-reaching and irreversible effects on the learning and achievement of children. Peske and Haycock (2006) noted research by William Sanders that found that, on average, low-achieving students gained about 14 percentage points each year of the Tennessee state test when taught by the least effective teachers, but more than 53 points when taught by the most effective teachers. Peske and Haycock conclude that "addressing gaps in access to teacher quality is the most critical element of a successful education reform agenda" (p. 9).

Limited Preschool Attendance

Viadero (2000) reports that African American and Latino children have less access to good preschool and day-care programs than do their white and Asian American counterparts. Preschool experiences develop important social, emotional, physical, and cognitive readiness for school. Readiness gaps can lead to any number of learning delays that often go undetected or misdiagnosed, setting in motion a chain of learning and achievement lags for many poor and minority students.

Prejudice, Stereotype Threat, and Poor Student Self-Concept

Subtle and overt forms of racism and prejudice hinder relationships between students and teachers and impede learning. The more obvious one's cultural difference is, the greater are the chances one may experience prejudice or discrimination. Displays of bias are pernicious and create dynamics of communication and interaction that hinder the free exchange of ideas and experimentation that are part of learning.

Following his 1990 studies on the performance anxiety of his African American undergraduate students, Stanford University sociologist Claude Steele developed the concept of "stereotype threat" to explain why many students of color score low on tests. The students were anxious about fulfilling the negative stereotypes that others had about their racial group. Once threatened, these students may go on to "disidentify" with the academic task or downplay its importance (Ogbu, 1992; Ogbu & Matute-Bianchi, 1990; Steele, 1995). Steele and Ogbu's observations provide important information for equity-minded educators trying to understand the perceived reluctance of some students of color to engage in rigorous academic work.

Furthermore, Gay, as cited in McREL (2000), notes a link between self-confidence, effort, and academic success. Low achievers, regardless of ethnicity, tend to attribute low ability and failure to external factors outside of their control and often see no point in even trying. The failure to connect effort to success creates a vicious cycle in which failure begets failure, and students feel victimized by factors outside of their own helplessness. Marzano (1998) supports the notion that teachers need to help their students believe that they can maximize their ability and success through effort.

Low Teacher Expectations

Lowered educational and social expectations are a well-documented correlate to the underpreparation of children of color. Lowered performance expectations too often lead to diminished instructional resources in schools with high minority and high poverty enrollments. The recent example of *Williams vs. State of California* (Powers, 2004), a class-action suit filed on behalf of the state's underperforming children from poverty, is a glaring example of how lowered expectations lead to diminished educational resources and inadequate school facilities for students who are not expected to succeed anyway.

Competing Technology

Time spent with readily available and engaging electronic devices such as television, DVDs, iPods, Game Boys, cell phones, and text messaging can be a distraction to academic learning. Likewise, academic learning devoid of electronic applications or skill building makes academic learning seem irrelevant, outdated, useless, and obsolete. Educators who use technology for tutorial instruction are much less effective with students of color or poverty than are educators who use technology as a means for learning (i.e., productivity tools to communicate learning). There is abundant evidence documenting that students of color, students of poverty, and special education students have much more exposure to learning *from* technology, such as tutorials, than learning *with* technology as a critical thinking tool (Grunwald, 2002; Prensky, 2006; Solomon, Allen, & Resta, 2003).

Test Bias

The jury is still out on the question of cultural bias in standardized tests against certain groups, although most psychometrists agree there is no such thing as a "culture-free" test (Cattell, 1979; Pascale & Jakubovic, 1971; Zurcher, 1998). When standards, curriculum, resources, and tests align, the issue of test bias is justifiably a question of curriculum bias. Without a doubt much of the current curriculum excludes the stories and perspectives of many of our students. And when instructional practices do not reflect our students' learning and linguistic patterns and styles, it is easy to understand how some students are at a disadvantage in classrooms that employ one-size-fits-all instructional resources, strategies, pacing plans, and assessments.

Poverty

Latino children are twice as likely as their white and Asian American counterparts to be raised in poverty (Berliner, 2005; Viadero, 2000). Poverty correlates with inadequate health care and wellness. Furthermore, children in poverty are more likely to be exposed to environmental hazards such as pollution, lead-based paints, vermin infestation, and other safety risks, which, over time, compromise their standard of living and readiness to learn. The effects of poverty often last from generation to generation, sometimes exacerbating a culture of hopelessness and academic underperformance.

High Mobility

A common correlate to poverty is high transience from place to place as families seek improved jobs, crop harvesting opportunities, more affordable housing, or housing with relatives. Performance lags are common when students move from school to school, have to make new friends, and adjust to new teachers and schools and lessons that are often not in sequence with curriculum at previous schools. In addition, in schools with high turnovers, it is not uncommon for teachers to slow down the instructional pace for all students, including those who do not move. Over time, students whose instructional pacing was slowed down or interrupted because of moving will have found themselves lagging behind their more stable peers.

■ Reflection

Which factors contributing to the achievement gap have you noticed affecting learning and achievement at your school? What can you do to mitigate these conditions?

_____

_____

_____

_____

A Review of Common Themes and Best Practices That Correlate With Closing Learning, Access, and Educational Gaps

Under high pressure to improve the achievement scores of underperforming student groups, schools are undertaking serious efforts to narrow the achievement gap, and the stories behind several successes are beginning to emerge and converge. In the California State Department of Education (2000) conference paper, *Analysis of Convergence in the Research on High-Performing, High-Poverty Schools, California's Statewide System of School Support,* five important research strands were present in schools and districts making progress in closing learning and achievement gaps. The literature reviewed (Carter, 1970; Haycock, 2001; Johnson, 2002; Picucci, Callicoatte, Brownson, Kahlert, & Sobel, 2002; Reeves, 2000) represents many of the current best practices for closing achievement gaps and, although the specific strategies differ slightly from researcher to researcher, the convergence of critical factors led to these overarching principles to guide closing gaps in high-minority schools. A synthesis of the convergence of factors for closing gaps follows. Schools and districts who are successfully narrowing and closing gaps for underserved student groups do the following:

- focus on academic achievement as the highest priority of the school;
- engage all stakeholders in high-quality teaching and learning of rigorous standards;
- sustain collegial and collaborative faculty teamwork;
- maintain high expectations for student achievement;
- link staff development to teaching of standards;
- use state and local standards and accountability systems to drive improvement efforts and academic achievement;
- engage parents as partners in the learning of their children by creating family-like schools and school-like families;
- use research and data to promote continuous improvement;
- maintain safe and orderly school climates conducive to learning;
- develop and sustain strong site leadership;
- reallocate and develop resources to pursue and sustain the site's goals;
- extend instructional time and early interventions;
- persist through the chaos, setbacks, difficult times, and failure;
- frequently monitor student progress; and
- sustain academic results.

You may be thinking that the above strategies are easier said than done, that the devil is in the details. You may be asking, "How should I/we go about it? What should be our first step?" We believe that the question that should drive your efforts is not "how?" but "why?" and "for whom?" Block (2001) says that *the answer to "how" is "yes."* In other words, without full commitment to closing gaps from a critical mass of your staff and community, no strategy, no matter how good, will work. Where there is a commitment to better serve your students who need the most, and where resources are allocated to that end, success will be inevitable.

The work you are about to begin is not different work. It is work you have done before. You know how to do it; you are just going to do it from a different perspective or lens. You will come to see that many of your well-intentioned policies and practice have contributed to the gaps, and as you change your perspectives and the focus of the work, collaboration and success will follow.

■ Reflection

What challenges exist for your school in closing learning access and achievement gaps for your students? Describe the progress your school might be making in closing important learning access and achievement gaps for your students. What opportunities do you see within your own practice?

_____

_____

_____

_____

An Exhortation for Taking Personal and Collective Responsibility for Closing Educational Gaps

Our complicity in the neglect of the educational needs of identified groups of citizens has not been due to lack of information. From the popular press to government-commissioned studies to current, prominent journal articles, descriptions about the barriers to access have been abundantly available. Ralph Ellison, in his seminal work *The Invisible Man* (1952), provided the lens of an African American male that should have awakened our society. Although Ellison's novel was read widely in the 1950s, and it persists on many high school and college American literature reading lists, its message of *invisibility* appears not to have resonated with people in the dominant group. Tom Carter's (1970) studies conducted for the U.S. Civil Rights Commission documented the educational neglect directed toward Mexican Americans. And, in a recent issue of the *Phi Delta Kappan,* Starnes (2006) traces the history of neglect experienced by First Nations people and the importance of educators knowing the history and culture of students who are different from them.

Not to know about the achievement gap, whether it is from our lack of interest, lack of effort, faulty assumptions, or believing that all students have equal access to academic and social success, seems like benign neglect. Nevertheless, neglect is not so benign when it leads to gaps between groups of students simply because of their gender, their language status, or the color of their skin. Closing educational gaps between cultural and economic groups in this country is the most American of all of our efforts. To ignore the gaps and to blame lags in performance on the deficiencies of the groups themselves is to unravel the tapestry of democracy on which this nation was founded.

We find ourselves at the dawn of the 21st century with a spate of local, state, and federal reform initiatives designed to narrow and close learning, access, and the achievement gaps, the most controversial being the No Child Left Behind Act (2001). If many of these reform initiatives have any redeeming social value it is in their calling attention to the "elephant in the middle of the room" that institutional policymakers and educators have ignored for the past 50 years, namely, that children and youth from low-income, African American, Latino, People of the First Nations, and English-learning families lag in reading and mathematics achievement when compared to white and Asian middle-class students.

Culturally proficient educators will not continue to ignore the insidious undereducation of students from certain demographic groups. Rather, they will respond with what Fullan (2003) calls "the moral imperative" of examining and changing our practices. Culturally proficient educators understand that underperforming students have been *underserved* by our educational system. These educators know that conversations must shift from how students are *underperforming* to how all adult stakeholders are *underserving* students and families. This shift in perspective is the first step in developing a pedagogy for closing the gap, which above all must be a pedagogy of caring, a pedagogy steeped in our moral responsibility to unfold the democracy on which this country was founded.

The cornerstone of this pedagogy has to be our commitment to close educational gaps regardless of the challenges and regardless of the human and fiscal capital that will be required. We have to say yes to the challenge rather than continue to be stymied by "how do we do it?" Now for the first time in the history of U.S. education, educators are compelled to examine the underlying issue of human, capital, fiscal, community, and political resource differentials among schools that have resulted in the phenomenon of the achievement gap. Although some educators and policymakers across the country will continue to debate the merits and shortcomings of state and national efforts to close the achievement gap, a few good men and women like you will continue to confront the reality of our national shortcoming to educate all children to a high level by saying yes to the challenge, by taking some of the first steps outlined in this book.

The time has come for every educator, every parent, every stakeholder and citizen to decide if he will play a role in unfolding the democracy in a manner that is inclusive. NAEP achievement gap data (Perie et al., 2005) compel educators to play a key role in doing whatever it takes to ensure that our students function at high academic levels, function well in our increasingly diverse society, and have a palpable sense of their own and others' cultures.

■ Reflection

How will you engage your colleagues with the issue of responsibility and facilitate challenging conversations, data analysis, and action?

_____

_____

_____

_____

2

The Tools
of Cultural
Proficiency

*If you don't like something, change it; if you can't
change it, change the way you think about it.*

—Mary Engelbreit (2006)

Getting Centered

What do you do when you hear colleagues, parents, or community
members make derisive comments about members of cultural
groups different from yours? Think of the last time you chose not to
respond to such a comment. What were you feeling then? What do
you wish you had done? What would you like to learn to assist you in
being proactive in such situations?

_____

_____

_____

_____

As we reviewed in Chapter 1, achievement gaps are historical and persistent. If they are to be closed, well-intended and well-informed educators and laypersons must make concerted efforts. Our work, as the authors of this book, is to call us together to see the achievement gaps as *our* issue. As we emphasized in Chapter 1, the issue of the academic underperformance of children of poverty, African American, Latino, and First Nations students is not new information. We are adding to the conversation the perspective that when focusing on our practices as educators, we can make a difference for our students and their communities if we pay attention to who our students are and what their particular needs are, rather than to our needs or the needs of the school system.

The Lens of Cultural Proficiency

Cultural proficiency is about being effective in cross-cultural situations. In the context of this book, cultural proficiency is about educating all students to high levels through knowing, valuing, and using their cultural backgrounds, languages, and learning styles within the context of our teaching. A central tenet of cultural proficiency holds that change is an *inside-out* process in which a person is, first and foremost, a student of his own assumptions. One must be able to recognize one's own assumptions in order to retain those that facilitate culturally proficient actions and to change those that impede such actions. Similarly, educators apply this inside-out process to examine school policies and practices that either impede or facilitate cultural proficiency. It is this ability to examine one's self and organization that is fundamental to addressing achievement gap issues.

Cultural proficiency (Cross, Bazron, Dennis, & Isaacs, 1989; Lindsey, Nuri Robins, & Terrell, 2003; Lindsey, Roberts, & CampbellJones, 2005; Nuri Robins, Lindsey, Lindsey, & Terrell, 2006) provides a comprehensive, systemic structure for school leaders to discuss issues facing their schools. The four tools of cultural proficiency provide educators with the means to assess and change their own values and behaviors and a school's policies and practices in a way that serves our society. Cultural proficiency has little to do with the outcomes we intend with our policies and practices and everything to do with the outcomes we actually achieve. The cultural proficiency rubrics presented in Chapter 6 are an applied use of the tools of cultural proficiency and will help you examine the outcomes you are achieving. If your self-study leads you to data or outcomes that you find unacceptable, the tools of cultural proficiency will help you refocus the lens of your intentions to achieve outcomes that better serve the needs of your students.

The Four Tools of Cultural Proficiency

Cultural proficiency is a mindset; it embodies a worldview. For those who commit to culturally proficient practices it represents a paradigmatic shift from viewing others as problematic to viewing how one works with people different from one's self in a manner to ensure effective practices. Cultural proficiency comprises an interrelated set of four tools that, when used authentically, offers one the opportunity to improve one's own practice in service of others. The tools of cultural proficiency are **not** strategies or techniques. The tools provide you with the means by which to perform your professional responsibilities in a culturally proficient manner. Being culturally competent or proficient is exemplified by how one uses assessment data, delivers curriculum and instruction, interacts with parents and community members, or plans and uses professional development. You can perform tasks related to educator functions and never utter the phrase "cultural proficiency."

Effective use of the cultural proficiency rubrics presented in Chapter 6 is predicated on one's knowing and understanding the four tools of cultural proficiency (Cross et al., 1989; Lindsey et al., 2003; Nuri Robins et al., 2006). The tools of cultural proficiency—the guiding principles, the barriers, the continuum, and the essential elements—combine to provide you with a framework for analyzing your values and behaviors as well as your school's policies and practices.

In this section we summarize salient features of each of the tools and how they support the relevance and utility of the rubrics. The guiding principles and the barriers provided a context for development of the rubrics. The continuum and the essential elements are the axes used in constructing the rubrics.

- The guiding principles of cultural proficiency serve as an introduction for a person or organization to identify their **core values** as they relate to issues of diversity.
- The cultural proficiency continuum provides **language to describe unhealthy and healthy** *values and behaviors* of persons and *policies and practices* of organizations. In addition, the

continuum can help you assess your current state and project your desired state. Movement along the continuum represents a shift in thinking from holding the view of *tolerating diversity* to *transformation for equity.* This is not a subtle shift in worldview; it is paradigmatic.

- The five essential elements of cultural competence serve as **standards** by which one develops healthy individual values or behaviors and organizational policies or practices.
- A section on identifying the barriers to cultural proficiency provides persons and their organizations with tools to overcoming resistance to change.

The Guiding Principles of Cultural Proficiency

The guiding principles provide a framework for the examination of the core values of schools and how espoused theory and theory in action differ when schools are undergoing academic self-study (Argyris, 1990; Schein, 1989). The guiding principles of cultural proficiency, and school-based examples of each principle, are as follows:

- Culture is a predominant force in people's and organization's lives.

  Illustrations: Holidays, religious observances, heroes, and sports interests are among examples of culture that affect educators, students, and parents.
- People are served in varying degrees by the dominant culture.

  Illustrations: Who is represented in the curriculum, is at the upper levels of achievement gaps, and has higher transition rates into colleges and universities are examples of those best served by the dominant culture. Likewise, it is dominant group members who predominate in the writing of curricular materials and provide the greatest number of educators.
- People have group identities and individual identities.

  Illustrations: Each educator, parent, guardian, student, and community member is an individual person with an identity that makes him unique. At the same time, he has gender identity and sexual orientation, may be a member of a religious group, knows his racial-ethnic background, and most likely is a member of formal and informal groups. In our elementary schools we know the second graders from the fifth graders. Likewise, in our secondary schools we can often distinguish the athletes from the French Club (though there may be some overlap).

- Diversity within cultures is vast and significant.

   Illustrations: Latino, African American, white, and Asian or Pacific Islander are all huge categories within which there are numerous ethnic groups, religious groups, gender groups, and social class groups, among others. Within school districts we often speak of the organizational cultural differences among schools or among the grade levels or departments within the same school.

- Each cultural group has unique cultural needs.

   Illustrations: Among the many cultural needs we experience in our schools are varied learning needs, different holidays to celebrate, and gender roles that differ. Among schools in the same district, we often find that the approaches to professional development differ when addressing elementary, middle, or high school educators.

What illustrations would you add?

_____

_____

_____

_____

Lindsey et al. (2005) noted that

understanding and acknowledging the five principles and choosing to manifest them in your behavior are demonstrations of culturally proficient leadership. The choice you make to align your leadership actions with the five principles of cultural proficiency communicates a strong message throughout your school's community that you value diversity and fully expect that every individual will do the same. Indeed, the guiding principles are attitudinal benchmarks that enable you and others to assess progress toward acknowledging and valuing cultural differences, and while this assessment yields crucial information, it is insufficient by itself in provoking the development of culturally proficient behaviors. (p. 52)

The guiding principles provide a framework for how the diversity of students informs professional practice in responding to student learning needs. If your school or district has a mission, vision, or beliefs statement, that is a good place to see if the stated values in your school align with predominant behaviors in the school. Most likely you will encounter phrases such as "all students," "valuing diversity," "twenty-first-century education," or "high-tech skills." Do leadership behaviors align with those expressed values?

_____

_____

_____

_____

The Continuum of Cultural Proficiency

The first three points of the continuum focus on *them* as being problematic (i.e., cultural destructiveness, cultural incapacity, cultural blindness), and the next three focus on *our practice* (i.e., cultural precompetence, cultural competence, cultural proficiency). The first three points may find us referring to our students as *underperforming*, whereas the next three points would find us referring to the ways in which we are *underserving* our students and their communities (the inside-out approach). Here are the six points of the continuum:

- Cultural destructiveness—Seeking to eliminate vestiges of the cultures of others.

  Illustrations: Historical examples include the system of slavery, westward expansion of the United States that resulted in the near-extinction of First Nations, and the presence of school curricula that seek to ignore these and other egregious acts in our history. Modern examples range from physical acts such as gay bashing to educational practices that perpetuate generational underachievement of demographic groups of students.
- Cultural incapacity—Seeking to make the culture of others appear to be wrong.

  Illustrations: Historical examples include legislation such as immigrant exclusion laws that severely curtailed Asian immigrants, the executive order that remanded U.S. citizens of Japanese ancestry into "relocation camps" during World War II, and law-based discriminatory hiring practices used throughout our country until the latter half of the 20th century. Current school-oriented examples include the expressed assumption that parents from some cultural groups don't care about their children's education if they don't come to school events or when educators exclaim they are successful when working with "normal kids."

- Cultural blindness—Refusing to acknowledge the culture of others.

  Illustrations: Historical examples include the failure to recognize, or even see, the artistic, athletic, economic, and political accomplishments of women, nondominant ethnic groups, and people who are gay or lesbian. In today's schools blindness is represented by our colleagues who profess "not to see color" or who were unaware of the achievement gaps until No Child Left Behind made them part of our conversation.

- Cultural precompetence—Being aware of what one doesn't know about working in diverse settings. Initial levels of awareness after which a person or organization can move in positive, constructive direction or they can falter, stop, and possibly regress.

  Illustrations: In our recent past there have been numerous attempts to address the needs of underachieving students that included "pull-out programs," gender-based academies, and ability grouping that led to "tracking." The distinguishing characteristic of educators who seek to learn how best to serve the needs of all students is that they do not perpetuate programs and approaches that fail to result in equitable outcomes but, rather, they continue to research, learn, and implement practices to serve all students.

- Cultural competence—Viewing one's personal and organizational work as an interactive arrangement in which the educator enters diverse settings in a manner that is additive to cultures that are different from the educator's.

  Illustrations: Examples include educators who acknowledge changing demographics in their schools and adapt the curriculum and instructional practices to "recognize and respond to the students in our classrooms today, not the ones who used to be here." In these classrooms and schools, culture is a normal part of educator conversation, language development strategies are employed as needed, and images of underrepresented groups abound even if they are not members of the current student population.

- Cultural proficiency—Making the commitment to lifelong learning for the purpose of being increasingly effective in serving the educational needs of cultural groups. Holding the vision of what can be and committing to assessments that serve as benchmarks on the road to student success.

    Illustrations: Educators who strive to achieve cultural proficiency recognize and value professional development, hold a value for social justice embodied in the attitude of "doing what is right for all students," and advocate for students and community groups as a normal part of their professional responsibility.

The Five Essential Elements of Cultural Competence

The elements are the second of the two tools used to construct each of the matrices. The essential elements become the standards for culturally competent values, behaviors, policies, and practices:

- Assessing cultural knowledge—Being aware of what you know about others' cultures, how you react to others' cultures, and what you need to do to be effective in cross-cultural situations.
- Valuing diversity—Making the effort to be inclusive of people whose viewpoints and experiences are different from yours and will enrich conversations, decision making, and problem solving.
- Managing the dynamics of difference—Viewing conflict as a natural and normal process that has cultural contexts that can be understood and can be supportive in creative problem solving.
- Adapting to diversity—Having the will to learn about others and the ability to use others' cultural experiences and backgrounds in educational settings.
- Institutionalizing cultural knowledge—Making learning about cultural groups and their experiences and perspectives an integral part of your ongoing learning.

Understanding Barriers to Cultural Proficiency

In the manner that the guiding principles provide a moral compass for culturally proficient actions, there are barriers to achieving culturally proficient actions. The barriers to cultural proficiency are

- resistance to change,
- systems of oppression, and
- a sense of entitlement.

These barriers are often manifested in statements such as, "It is not me who needs to change. I have been a successful educator for years; these kids/parents just need to get a clue!" Similarly, it is rare to find the person who doesn't acknowledge that racism, ethnocentrism, and sexism exist in our society, but what they often fail to see is that when one group of people loses rights and privileges because of systemic oppression, those rights and privileges accrue to others in often unacknowledged or unrecognized ways. It is when one recognizes one's entitlement that one has the ability to make choices that benefit the education of children and youth.

Most educational policymakers and educators, when focusing on the achievement issues of nondominant students, experience a conversation gap. The gap in conversation, often unrecognized and unacknowledged, is in educators not having the perspective to see roadblocks that have been, and are, placed in the way of members of nondominant socioeconomic, racial, ethnic, gender, or language groups. This selective invisibility leads to a sense of privilege and entitlement for members of the dominant group. Whereas systems of oppression impose barriers for members of nondominant groups, concomitant systems of privilege and entitlement impose barriers for members of the dominant group. The barriers erected by a sense of privilege and entitlement involve a skewed sense of reality that can impede one's ability to pursue ethical and moral avenues in meeting the academic and social needs of nondominant groups.

The position of privilege often fosters educators voicing biased or ill-informed assumptions about parents from nondominant groups. Typical of such assumptions are comments such as

"Their parents won't come to parent conferences because they don't care about the education of their child."

"Why try to help them? They will just end up as gang bangers, just like their dad!"

"Why should I learn anything about their culture? This is America; let them learn about us!"

Educators who make comments like those above are in need of different lenses, tools, and structures to understand their students, the barriers they face, and the special learning needs they have in order to be successful in school. Educators must engage in intentional conversations about how parents and students who are different from them behave and learn. Cultural proficiency is an approach for bringing to the surface assumptions and values that undermine the success of some student groups and a lens for examining how we can include and honor the cultures and learning needs of all students in the educational process.

■ Reflection

How comfortable are you with your knowledge of cultural proficiency? What questions do you have? What more do you want to learn about the tools of cultural proficiency? How do you see the tools of cultural proficiency helping you and members of your school community narrow and close educational achievement gaps?

_____

_____

_____

_____

Further Reading

If you would like to read more about the tools of cultural proficiency, here are some suggested topics and readings.

The Guiding Principles of Cultural Proficiency

Kikanza Nuri Robins, Randall B. Lindsey, Delores B. Lindsey, and Raymond D. Terrell (2006). *Culturally Proficient Instruction: A Guide for People Who Teach* (2nd ed.). Thousand Oaks, CA: Corwin Press, pages 17–24.

Randall B. Lindsey, Laraine M. Roberts, and Franklin CampbellJones (2005). *The Culturally Proficient School: An Implementation Guide for School Leaders.* Thousand Oaks, CA: Corwin Press, pages 17–50.

Randall B. Lindsey, Kikanza Nuri Robins, and Raymond D. Terrell (2003). *Cultural Proficiency: A Manual for School Leaders* (2nd ed.). Thousand Oaks, CA: Corwin Press, pages 159–165.

The Cultural Proficiency Continuum

Kikanza Nuri Robins, Randall B. Lindsey, Delores B. Lindsey, and Raymond D. Terrell (2006). *Culturally Proficient Instruction: A Guide for People Who Teach* (2nd ed.). Thousand Oaks, CA: Corwin Press, pages 77–105.

Randall B. Lindsey, Laraine M. Roberts, and Franklin CampbellJones (2005). *The Culturally Proficient School: An Implementation Guide for School Leaders.* Thousand Oaks, CA: Corwin Press, pages 53–78.

Randall B. Lindsey, Kikanza Nuri Robins, and Raymond D. Terrell (2003). *Cultural Proficiency: A Manual for School Leaders* (2nd ed.). Thousand Oaks, CA: Corwin Press, pages 84–91.

The Essential Elements of Cultural Competence

Kikanza Nuri Robins, Randall B. Lindsey, Delores B. Lindsey, and Raymond D. Terrell (2006). *Culturally Proficient Instruction: A Guide for People Who Teach* (2nd ed.). Thousand Oaks, CA: Corwin Press, pages 39–50, 107–188.

Randall B. Lindsey, Laraine M. Roberts, and Franklin CampbellJones (2005). *The Culturally Proficient School: An Implementation Guide for School Leaders.* Thousand Oaks, CA: Corwin Press, pages 87–102.

Randall B. Lindsey, Kikanza Nuri Robins, and Raymond D. Terrell (2003). *Cultural Proficiency: A Manual for School Leaders* (2nd ed.). Thousand Oaks, CA: Corwin Press, pages 112–122.

Barriers to Cultural Proficiency

Kikanza Nuri Robins, Randall B. Lindsey, Delores B. Lindsey, and Raymond D. Terrell (2006). *Culturally Proficient Instruction: A Guide for People Who Teach* (2nd ed.). Thousand Oaks, CA: Corwin Press, pages 59–76.

Randall B. Lindsey, Laraine M. Roberts, and Franklin CampbellJones (2005). *The Culturally Proficient School: An Implementation Guide for School Leaders.* Thousand Oaks, CA: Corwin Press, pages 103–124.

Randall B. Lindsey, Kikanza Nuri Robins, and Raymond D. Terrell (2003). *Cultural Proficiency: A Manual for School Leaders* (2nd ed.). Thousand Oaks, CA: Corwin Press, pages 217–230, 244–271.

Part II

Knowing the Demographics of Your School

Culturally Proficient
Inquiry Is Guided By Knowledge

T he second part of this book is organized to facilitate your understanding of your school serving the needs of all students. We educators, until recently, have not made the achievement gap central to our work. In these chapters we put a face on the achievement gap by graphically demonstrating who is well served by prevailing educational practices and who is not well served; hence, the educational dynamic known as *the achievement gap*.

In Part II we describe how you can study your own school by identifying what is working well and areas where improvement is needed. It is to be noted that we use a consistent frame of reference throughout the book, *your school*. You can apply the tools in this book to your classroom, your grade level, your department, your school, your regional cluster of schools, or your school district. Figure II.1 on the following page builds on the information in Figure I.1 in the Part 1 introduction, serves to introduce Chapters 3 to 6, and develops a context for the value, importance, and limitations of data.

Chapter 3 has two primary purposes—to use NAEP 2004 data to frame national trends in student achievement, and to describe the Peer Group Model for local school assessment and planning. Chapter 4 describes how demographic variables in data are fundamental to informed discussions focused on closing the achievement gaps. For many educators with whom we work, discussing demographic data provokes uncomfortable, even angry responses. Such reactions are commonplace in our schools and are usually indications of the need for dialogue to take place. This chapter equips you with these important pieces of information:

- The Peer Group Model for use in comparing demographic groups in order to change educational practices when needed.
- Where and how to find relevant data in your school or district with little effort.
- Standards-assessment data and norm-referenced achievement test data.
- Behavioral and program access measures that provide a comprehensive picture of how demographic groups of students are faring at your school.
- Ways to identify the types of information you will collect about students attending your school.

Chapter 5 provides an overview of the step-by-step process for planning and conducting the Cultural Proficiency Inquiry, an in-depth self-study. Chapter 6 presents four rubrics as leverage points for creating systemic change in your school:

- Assessment and Accountability,
- Curriculum and Instruction,
- Parent and Community Communication and Outreach, and
- Professional Development.

Figure II.1   Culturally Proficient Inquiry

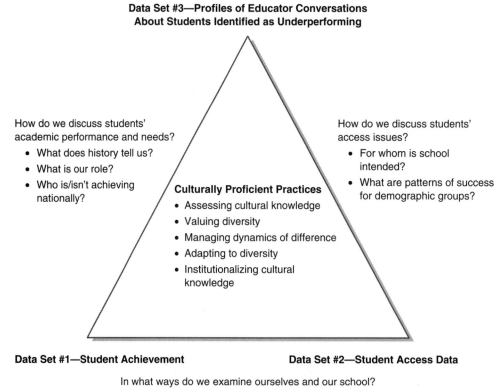

Data Set #3—Profiles of Educator Conversations About Students Identified as Underperforming

How do we discuss students' academic performance and needs?
- What does history tell us?
- What is our role?
- Who is/isn't achieving nationally?

Culturally Proficient Practices
- Assessing cultural knowledge
- Valuing diversity
- Managing dynamics of difference
- Adapting to diversity
- Institutionalizing cultural knowledge

How do we discuss students' access issues?
- For whom is school intended?
- What are patterns of success for demographic groups?

Data Set #1—Student Achievement   Data Set #2—Student Access Data

In what ways do we examine ourselves and our school?
- How congruent are our practices?
- What are the national trends?

3

NAEP Data Show the Way, With Limitations

There are three kinds of lies: lies, damned lies, and statistics.

—Benjamin Disraeli

Think of the ways in which you and your colleagues use data in classrooms, grade level or departments, schools, or the district to make informed decisions. What kinds of kind of data do you use? What decisions derive from your analysis of your data?

Please use the space below to record your response.

_____

_____

_____

_____

It would be unusual to find an educator who hasn't heard or repeated the seemingly cynical epigraph above. As consumers we are exposed to sales pitches represented as scientifically based claims for the best bath soap, the highest performing automobile, and the best song to represent the "X" generation. Our consumer-oriented society has made many of us suspicious about the use, and misuse, of statistics. Used correctly, however, statistics can support you in making confident everyday and long-range decisions that affect the lives of our students.

With this chapter, we introduce the manner in which the achievement gap is quantified, interpreted, and presented. To understand the achievement gap, one must be able to analyze and use statistical data, interpret data in order to make responsible educational decisions, and set goals for closing the achievement gap. With this in mind, this chapter helps deepen your knowledge about two issues that are fundamental to understanding and successfully confronting the achievement gap:

- important historical and current data from the National Association of Education Progress (NAEP), which document academic achievement gaps among defined demographic groups; and
- the effect size statistic, which provides a means for knowing the magnitude, or extent, of achievement gaps between identified demographic groups.

Who Does the Achievement Gap Affect?

In reality, our schools work relatively well for the students for whom the schools were designed several generations ago, whereas the same schools struggle in trying to serve all other students (Edwards, 2006; Wartell & Huelskamp, 1991). Students most negatively affected in this equation are nondominant groups of students—poor students, English learners, and African American, Latino, and First Nations students.

That the disparities are rooted in racist, ethnocentric, and sexist contexts of the past and present, as discussed in Chapter 1, is rarely discussed in policymaking or educational circles. To fully address the academic achievement gap that persists in our schools, it is necessary to be mindful of the gaps in our own knowledge as educators, such as those represented in Chapter 1.

Ample literature (Haycock, 2001; Perie et al., 2005) exists to document the historical and current academic achievement gap between African American, Latino, and white students. The literature describes the achievement gap using student achievement indicators such as national standards-based assessments, state testing standards, norm-referenced assessments, and college entrance examinations. In Chapter 4 we identify access gaps among student demographic groups that serve to compound issues of underachievement.

■ NAEP Provides the Big Picture

The value of the National Assessment of Educational Progress (NAEP) is that it provides a current and historical, "big-picture" look at how identified demographic groups perform over time. The NAEP has been administered nationwide since 1971. It is a standards-based test that measures reading, mathematics, and writing skills. The NAEP monitors the progress of various groups of students to determine whether any change in national scores is occurring across student groups or is limited to a particular group.

The NAEP is administered to a national representative group of 9-, 13-, and 17-year-old students. It offers demographic group comparisons by gender, ethnicity, poverty, and parent educational level. The ethnic groups are limited to the African American, Latino, and white demographic groups and, because of small national sample sizes, do not at this time include Asian, Pacific Islander, First Nations, or Filipino students.

■ NAEP 2004 Quantified the Achievement Gap

The NAEP 2004 (Perie, 2005) study found statistically significant achievement gaps between white and African American students, between white and Latino students, and between poverty and nonpoverty students. We have selected key NAEP 2004 findings to guide our explanation of the complexity of the achievement gap and its underlying issues. Some of the more relevant findings are the following:

1. A statistically significant difference between African American and white students was noted in reading, mathematics, and writing at grades 4, 8, and 12. African American students scored significantly below white students.

2. A statistically significant difference between Latino and white students was noted in reading, mathematics, and writing at grades 4, 8, and 12. Latino students scored significantly below white students.

3. A statistically significant difference between students from poverty and nonpoverty settings was noted in reading, mathematics, and writing at grades 4, 8, and 12. Students of poverty scored significantly below the nonpoverty students.

4. A statistically significant difference between male and female students was noted in writing at grades 4, 8, and 12 and in reading at grades 8 and 12. In all cases males scored significantly below female students.

The above statistically significant differences are not unique to the 2004 assessment. These achievement gaps are evident and historical. So, as we indicated in Chapter 1, we in the educational community have been apprised of the existence of the achievement gap for more than three decades! A limitation of the above-reported findings is that we have no idea of the magnitude, or extent, of the achievement gap for any of these groups of students, only that a gap exists.

You can review these long-term trends by visiting the NAEP Web site at http://nces.ed.gov/nationsreportcard.

■ From the 2004 NAEP, the Story of Inequity Emerges

Examination of the 2004 NAEP results provides historical and current documentation of the achievement gap and puts faces on our students in terms of their gender, ethnicity, and poverty groupings. The findings from these studies demonstrate the significance of the student achievement gap at the national level, but NOT the magnitude or extent of these achievement gaps among demographic groups. In order to make the most meaning from this information, it is important to begin by describing criteria that establish significant differences between groups.

This may lead you to ask the very practical question, "why should I be concerned about statistical significance, and what does it mean anyway?" The response to this question is practical, not rhetorical. There are two prominent statistical measures to know and understand:

1. Tests of statistical significance attest to the existence of achievement gaps based on a probability model.

2. Tests of effect size or magnitude of difference are more practical for school site use and are used to describe achievement differences between any two demographic groups of students.

> We use the term "educational significance" to describe a practical, meaningful educational difference between groups and to express the extent or magnitude of the difference.

Used together, statistical significance and educational significance provide educators with more powerful tools to analyze the current levels of student achievement, to plan curricular and instructional programs, to identify benchmarks for progress, and to mark annual progress.

■ Is There a Gap? NAEP Reveals *Existence* of Achievement Gaps

The NAEP results reported to schools and media use **tests of statistical significance** to reveal the existence of achievement gaps. Tests of statistical significance typically compare large group mean scores (i.e., like those found in large research projects) to determine whether the difference between two groups represents actual differences. This approach has two limitations:

- These comparisons involve large sample sizes, typically found in national, state, or large district studies such as those in the NAEP study. This can create statistically significant differences between two groups, but the actual difference may have no practical relevance in an educational setting. For example, you may find a statistical difference in the reading achievement scores of the fourth-grade students in two schools in your district, even though students in both schools are reading at grade level.
- Large-scale studies such as the NAEP are limited in demographic analyses and may not include groups in your school such as English learners, Asian and Pacific Islanders, or People of the First Nations.

Although these data and tests of statistical difference have their value in regional and state-level comparisons, they have little practical effect at school sites or within most school districts. Unfortunately, the *national* method tends to be more popular in educational research literature and often leads to distorted interpretations of findings. However, the good news is that the educationally significant effect size measure of magnitude of difference provides accessible information for school-site decision makers. For ease of reading, from this point forward we use the phrase "extent of difference" to be equivalent to the magnitude or strength of difference.

■ How Big or Little Is the Gap? The *Extent* of Achievement Gaps

The second method is the use of the *effect size statistic.* What is an effect size? The effect size is a measure of the difference between two groups expressed in standard deviation units. **Tests of effect size** (also called "magnitude of difference") reveal the size of, or the *extent* of, achievement gaps. Effect size reports the extent of the difference between the two groups; it is less dependent on sample size and therefore more useful at school sites. Effect size can be used with large and small sample sizes with professional confidence.[1]

Your next question may be, "What is a good criterion when examining effect size?" For educational purposes, we recommend an effect size of 0.25. We consider an effect size of 0.25 or more between groups to be educationally significant. As we mentioned above, "educationally significant" refers to a difference that has practical, educational implications for determining performance gaps between groups. To make effect size a more usable statistic, Marzano, Pickering, and Pollock (2001) convert effect sizes into a *mean percentile gain score.* An effect size of 0.25 represents a mean percentile gain of 10 percentile points. Effect size is also used to determine educationally significant differences in student access data, as you will see in Chapters 8 and 9.[2]

■ NAEP Data and the *Extent of Difference* Between Groups—Effect Size Analysis

In order to understand the nature of the achievement gaps between demographic groups and for local schools to establish priorities to them, we must understand the extent of the gaps. Although NAEP data clearly point out the existence of achievement gaps, our local schools need data that we can use to make decisions about curriculum and instruction priorities.

NAEP data for 2004 are illustrated in Graphs 3.1–3.4. We provide effect size analysis to demonstrate educationally significant achievement gaps for the demographic groups reported in the NAEP. The tables report grade-level effect sizes at fourth, eighth, and 12th grades for African American and white students, Latino and white students,

---

1. The effect size approach is recommended by the American Psychological Association (1994) as a relevant method for interpreting differences between groups and is more useful in analyzing data for practical use at your school.

2. Further discussion of the rationale for establishing the effect size at 0.25 and the value of effect sizes is included in the Appendix.

poverty and nonpoverty students, and male and female students. The analyses reported in the following graphs, unfortunately, consistently illustrate negative values. Negative values indicate that African American and Latino students scored below white students, poverty students scored below nonpoverty students, and males scored below female students on these measures. To make the graphs reader friendly, effect sizes are reported only where there were statistically significant differences as reported in the NAEP data. In keeping with the discussion above, an effect size of 0.25 (i.e., 10 percentile gain or greater) is considered an educationally significant difference between two groups.

Graph 3.1 illustrates the analyses for fourth-grade students taking the most recent NAEP test. We note several observations of educationally significant differences:

- Lower performance in reading, mathematics, and writing is noted for African American and Latino students when compared to white students.
- Lower performance in reading, mathematics, and writing is noted for students of poverty when compared to nonpoverty students.
- Lower performance in writing is noted for male students when compared to female students.

As indicated above and for ease of interpretation, effect sizes can be converted to mean percentile gain scores (Marzano et al., 2001). An effect size of 0.25 represents a 10-point mean percentile difference between two groups. Table 3.1 provides the conversion of effect sizes to mean percentile scores.

Graph 3.1   Grade 4 NAEP Results

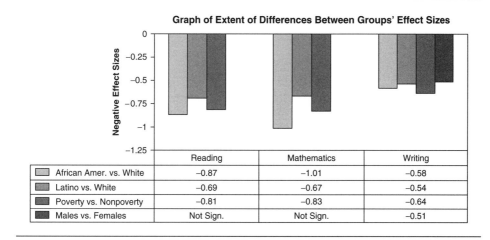

	Reading	Mathematics	Writing
African Amer. vs. White	−0.87	−1.01	−0.58
Latino vs. White	−0.69	−0.67	−0.54
Poverty vs. Nonpoverty	−0.81	−0.83	−0.64
Males vs. Females	Not Sign.	Not Sign.	−0.51

Table 3.1   Effect Size and Comparable Percentile Scores

Effect Size	Percentile Gain Difference
0.00	0
0.10	4
0.20	8
0.25	10
0.30	12
0.40	16
0.50	19
0.65	24
0.80	29
1.00	34
1.50	43
2.00	48

Percentile scores are usually more familiar to educators and to laypersons. Again, turning to Graph 3.1, we can make these observations:

- Effect size scores for African American students compared with white students illustrate that African American students test scores in reading, mathematics, and writing far exceeded the educationally significant effect size of 0.25 (i.e., 10 percentile points) and, in fact, exceeded 0.58 (i.e., a 22 percentile point difference) in all tests.
- Effect size scores for Latino students compared to white students and for students of poverty compared to nonpoverty students demonstrate achievement gaps greater than an effect size of .54, or 21 percentile point difference, in reading, mathematics, and writing.
- The greatest difference in effect sizes were in mathematics:
  - African American students' mean scores were an effect size of −1.01, or 34 percentile points lower than those of white students;
  - Latino students' mean scores were an effect size of −0.67, or 25 percentile points lower than those of white students; and
  - mean scores for students from poverty were an effect size of −0.83, or 30 percentile points below those of white students.

- Educationally significant differences were not noted between male and female students in reading and mathematics.

These data indicate that current practices are not having equitable results for these two groups of students. In such cases, effect size assists in identifying the extent or magnitude of differences by subject area, which is critical in curriculum program planning.

As you will see in Chapter 7, this analysis of effect size when applied to standards-based assessments allows you to pinpoint how well students are being served by current practices.

Graph 3.2 provides analysis for eighth-grade students taking the most recent NAEP test. Negative values indicate lower performance for African American and Latino students compared to white students, for students from poverty compared to nonpoverty students, and for male students compared to female students. As with fourth-grade students, eighth-grade white students outperformed African American and Latino students by an effect size of 0.66 or an average 25 percentile points or more in reading, mathematics, and writing. The same was true of nonpoverty students compared to students from poverty backgrounds, with the lowest effect size of 0.71, or 26 percentile points, in writing.

Educationally significant differences are not noted between male and female students in mathematics but are noted in reading and writing effect sizes exceeding 0.30 (i.e., 12 percentile points or greater).

The fourth-grade pattern in mathematics continued into the eighth grade. This pattern was even more pronounced for African American and Latino students. African American students' mean scores were greater than an effect size of −1.12, or 37 percentile points, below those of white students; Latino mean scores were an effect size of −0.82, or 29 percentile points, below those of white students; and poverty students' mean scores were an effect size of −0.87, or 31 percentile points, below those of white students.

Graph 3.3 provides analysis for 12th-grade students taking the most recent NAEP test. Consistent with fourth- and eighth-grade results, African American and Latino students when compared to the white students demonstrated an effect size of 0.56 or greater (i.e., 21 percentile points or more) in reading and mathematics, and an effect size of 0.46 or greater (i.e., 18 percentile points or more) in writing.

Students from poverty backgrounds when compared to nonpoverty students demonstrated an effect size difference of 0.46 or greater (i.e., 18 percentile points or more) in reading, mathematics, and writing.

Graph 3.2 Grade 8 NAEP Results

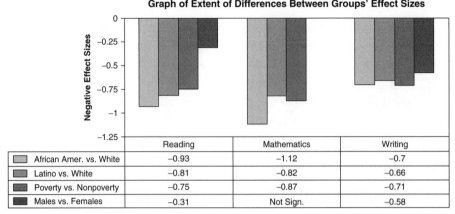

Graph of Extent of Differences Between Groups' Effect Sizes

	Reading	Mathematics	Writing
African Amer. vs. White	−0.93	−1.12	−0.7
Latino vs. White	−0.81	−0.82	−0.66
Poverty vs. Nonpoverty	−0.75	−0.87	−0.71
Males vs. Females	−0.31	Not Sign.	−0.58

Graph 3.3 Grade 12 NAEP Results

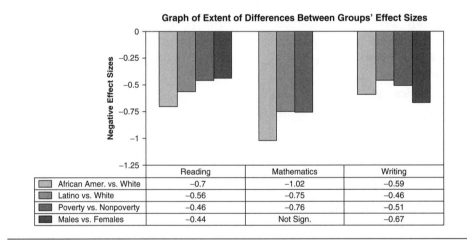

Graph of Extent of Differences Between Groups' Effect Sizes

	Reading	Mathematics	Writing
African Amer. vs. White	−0.7	−1.02	−0.59
Latino vs. White	−0.56	−0.75	−0.46
Poverty vs. Nonpoverty	−0.46	−0.76	−0.51
Males vs. Females	−0.44	Not Sign.	−0.67

Educationally significant differences were not noted between male and female students in mathematics, but consistent with eighth-grade performance there was an educationally significant difference with an effect size of −0.67 (a difference of 25 percentile points) in writing favoring female students' compared to male students' performance.

Table 3.2 converts the effect sizes in Graphs 3.1–3.3 to their mean percentile gain scores. This conversion is included for Grades 4, 8, and 12 and is noted only when there were statistically significant differences between groups as identified in the NAEP study. Educationally significant effect sizes are reported only if there were statistically significant differences between groups on the NAEP. Based on an effect size of 0.25, any mean percentile score of 10 or greater in Table 3.1 is considered to be an educationally significant

Table 3.2   Extent of Achievement Gap: Mean Percentile Differences by Race, Ethnicity, Poverty, and Gender

	2004 NAEP Study		
Groups Compared	*Grade 4*	*Grade 8*	*Grade 12*
African American and White			
Reading	31	32	26
Mathematics	34	37	35
Writing	22	26	22
Hispanic/Latino and White			
Reading	26	29	21
Mathematics	25	29	27
Writing	21	25	18
Poverty and Nonpoverty			
Reading	29	27	18
Mathematics	30	31	28
Writing	24	26	20
Males and Females			
Reading	N.S.*	12	17
Mathematics	N.S.*	N.S.*	N.S.*
Writing	20	22	25

*N.S. No statistically significant difference between demographic groups as determined by the NAEP.

difference between the groups. The mathematics achievement gap is consistent at all three age levels on the NAEP. Twelfth-grade African American students' mean scores resulted in an effect size of −1.02, or 34 percentile points, lower than those of white students; Latino mean scores resulted in an effect size of −0.75, or 27 percentile points, lower than those of white students; and poverty students mean scores resulted in an effect size of −0.76, or 28 percentile points, lower than those of nonpoverty students.

Again, this information provides important information for establishing instructional priorities.

■ Summary of Findings From NAEP Data

Analysis of Table 3.2 yields these observations:

African American Students

African American students have the largest achievement gap in reading and mathematics at Grades 4, 8, and 12 when compared to the other groups. In mathematics, the typical African American student scores 34 percentile points below the average white students at all three grade levels. African American students' scores represent educationally significant differences by scoring below white students in writing, but are more similar to the other groups in the extent of their learning gap.

Latino Students

Latino students generally score between the African American and poverty students. This was evident at Grade 4 for reading, mathematics, and writing; at Grade 8 in mathematics and writing; and at Grade 12 in writing. The average Latino student scores approximately 21–29 percentile points below white students across the subject areas and grades assessed.

Poverty Students

Students from poverty backgrounds demonstrated the largest achievement gap of the groups in writing at Grade 4. They generally demonstrated the second largest achievement gaps in reading and mathematics, which were less than that for African American students and more than that for Latino students. The average student from a background of poverty scores 30 percentile points below the nonpoverty group of students in mathematics and 18 to 29 percentile points below nonpoverty students in reading.

Gender Differences

Female students score higher than male students in writing at Grades 4, 8, and 12. The largest achievement gap in writing for all three grade levels was between females and males at the 12th grade, with the average female scoring 25 percentile points above the average male student.

■ Summary of Contribution of Effect Size With NAEP Data

The NAEP study indicated only statistically significant differences between groups, and the application of the effect size approach indicated the extent or magnitude of these differences. Some observations in using the effect size analysis applied to NAEP data are as follows:

African American and White Students

- Of the demographic groups compared, African American students had the greatest achievement gap when compared to white students in reading, mathematics, and writing.
- The achievement gap in mathematics is most extensive between African American and white students.
- African American students demonstrated similar levels of achievement gaps in writing when compared to white students as did the other demographic groups.

Poverty Students

- Poverty students followed African American students in experiencing the next largest achievement gaps in reading, mathematics, and writing.
- It is interesting to note that the poverty student reading achievement gap lessened from fourth to 12th grade.

Latino and White Students

- Latino students demonstrated less of an achievement gap when compared to African American students overall and, for most of the grade level tests, to poverty students.
- Latino students showed their largest achievement gaps at grades 4 and 8, especially in mathematics.

Tests of Significant Difference—Our *Both/And* Position

It is not an either-or world when working with issues as important as the education of our children and youth. Tests of statistically significant difference have informed us on national and local stages of the existence of educational achievement gaps. Furthermore, such tests confirm who are benefiting from current educational practices and who are not being served well by current practice. Tests of educational significance provide more useful information for local school use in that they inform the extent of achievement gaps, thereby providing solid baseline information by which educators can craft policies and practices that can be assessed and modified in an ongoing fashion.

Information provided by the effect size analysis offers educators usable and useful information in understanding the dynamics of the achievement gap and in establishing educational priorities. Chapter 4 applies the peer group model by providing descriptions of student achievement and student access data that will supply you and your colleagues with a more detailed picture of the students who are succeeding and the students who are struggling in your school.

■ Reflection

Take a few moments to think about these data. What variables in the data stand out for you? Which students are lagging behind? What does the term "educationally significant difference" mean to you?

_____

_____

_____

_____

4

The Peer Group Model— Achievement and Access Data

Learning without thought is labour lost.

—Confucius

What data inform you about the performance of your students? How do you make a determination that a student is not doing well or *under-performing?* What student achievement data are available to you?

_____

_____

_____

_____

From your reading to this point you know the dimensions of the achievement gap that confronts us as a society and as a profession. In Chapter 1, you learned that the achievement gap is historical, can be measured, and has demographic characteristics. In Chapter 2, you learned that the tools of cultural proficiency support your quest to ensure that all students have access to a high-quality education. Chapter 3 showed that the achievement gap has been documented since 1971 and used statistical measures to describe the enormity of achievement gaps. This chapter helps you learn what data to collect about your students and how to analyze those data using the *peer group model* to determine the significance of the gaps between student demographic groups.

What Do You Want to Know About Students in Your School?

In this chapter, you will learn an appropriate way to organize data about demographic groups of students for studying achievement gaps, to select appropriate test scores to use in your school study, and to select other sources of information available at your school or district that will provide a well-rounded analysis.

Part III that follows presents a protocol for you to use in collecting and analyzing your student information, examples of demographic group data for you to review, and guidelines for determining demographic group performance.

■ Assessing Achievement Gaps—Assets and Limitations

Disaggregating student information enables you to have a better understanding of students' educational needs and to avoid making inappropriate generalizations about groups of students. The identification of student demographic groups at your school is a critical discussion to have with your colleagues. The information you collect will be valid only if you are able to disaggregate student achievement data.

National and state-level directives for assessment and accountability provide readily identifiable demographic groups to use in school-level studies. Assessment data used in schools are often disaggregated by

- gender,
- race-ethnicity,
- social class (e.g., a commonly used indicator is student participation in free- and reduced-price lunch programs; parent education level is used on occasion),

- special education classification, and
- English-language fluency.

One can scan an assessment report and identify which demographic groups of students are performing better than others. Usually two types of analyses can be made:

- an achievement gap between a demographic group of students and a preset norm (e.g., how students of poverty compare to a normed test for fourth-grade reading), and
- an achievement gap between two demographic groups of students (e.g., how Latino students compare to African American students in 10th grade mathematics).

Two common practices, each with important limitations, are used to compare student demographic groups achievement gaps:

- to contrast achievement gaps between white and other ethnic groups, and
- to include individual students in overlapping groups (nondichotomous or discrete groups) when making demographic groups comparisons. For example, an English-learning Latino student is often represented in two demographic groups—a member of the demographic group, Latino, and a member of the demographic group of English learners.

Both data sorts present a distorted picture of student achievement. These approaches are distorted because they combine one or more student demographic groups into a single group, making it difficult to identify the learning needs of each specific group. This approach can lead to inappropriate generalizations for specific demographic groups combined in the total group.

The Limitation of Comparing Ethnic Groups

A primary example of comparing ethnic achievement gaps is the national standards-based NAEP study we discussed in Chapter 3. The NAEP study compares student achievement between white students and African American students and between white students and Latino students. This procedure establishes the white group as the sole reference point for the discussion of the achievement gap. The validity of using white student performance as the standard represents a cultural bias that white students outperform other cultural groups and that white students represent the majority population of students within a school, district, or state. We are well aware from the literature (Haycock, 2001) and our personal experiences that these assumptions do not apply to educational settings uniformly throughout the United States. These assumptions do not hold true in the following contexts:

- in settings where scores for high-performing students are not compared to other groups because of their small sample size (e.g., Asian students are not reported in the NAEP study), and
- in districts or schools with very diverse student populations, as in states such as California where 31% of students are white.

Therefore, it is incumbent on us as educators to use measures that provide information that we can use to select and modify curricular and instructional practices that best serve the students in our schools. The peer group model, described below, presents such information to practitioners.

Limitations of Demographic Group and Total Student Comparisons

It is common to find student demographic group achievement compared to the total student achievement at a school, district, or state level. Such comparisons are not particularly helpful for school-site use. For example, when analyzing Latino student achievement, Latino student achievement is frequently compared to all students or the total achievement scores of the grade, school, or district. This procedure is not an accurate comparison of Latino student achievement because Latino students are included in both groups. A more accurate comparison is to remove the Latino students from the total group score so we are truly comparing Latino achievement to the rest of the school or district population. A more obvious example may be the comparisons between males and females. One would not compare male student performance to all students because males would be included in both groups. It is easy to see in this example that male performance comparisons would be distorted. Instead, we compare males to females, two discrete groups.

■ The Peer Group Model

We recommended that demographic group comparisons be made with their *peer* group at the district or school. The peer group model compares students in one group to all other students (i.e., their peers) at your school. For example, an African American student's peer group is all non-African American students in the school. The peer group model approach represents a more valid comparison of student achievement gaps within a school or district or social context. This context is reflective of local student demographics and incorporates more of the student population in the achievement gap analysis. Some examples of useful demographic group comparisons include the following:

- White students to nonwhite students
- African American students to non-African American students
- Latino students to non-Latino students
- Students from low-income households to middle-class students
- Male students to female students

English Learners as a Demographic Group

The goal in arraying student test data is to provide you with data in a fashion that is useful for you in meeting the academic needs of your students. English learners are typically included in comparison groups for student achievement instead of being considered as a separate group with unique learning needs. This creates an unequal playing field by comparing groups who are predominantly English speaking to groups that include non-English-speaking students. For example, when evaluating Latino achievement gaps, Latino English learners are also included in the Latino population. This type of analysis does not acknowledge the unique learning needs of English learners, including the types of measures used to assess their English language development.

Inclusion of non-English speakers' tests administered in English has the effect of lowering student performance levels for all Latinos, especially in English language arts tests. Inclusion of English learners is, therefore, not reflective of the achievement levels of English-speaking Latino students who are in our core instructional programs. Depending on your school's demographics, the ethnic groups most frequently affected by including English learners are Asian American and Latino students. This also may be a factor from some schools with larger numbers of English-speaking students from Eastern Europe. Similarly, inclusion of English learners can distort achievement comparisons for gender and for poverty and nonpoverty students.

We strongly recommend when you have a population of English learners in your school that you disaggregate their test data from total school or grade-level data in order to provide you with the most reliable information for both the English learners and the balance of your student population. For example, if you seek to know how well fourth-grade Latino students are performing on a mathematics standards-based assessment, it is best to disaggregate Latino students designated as English learners from all other fourth-grade students. This provides you with more accurate and usable data for both the English learner students as well as for the fluent English-speaking students. Also, by disaggregating the English-learning students' scores from the rest of the fourth-grade students, you don't inadvertently combine fluent English-speaking Latino students with the English-learning population and thereby make a miscalculation regarding English-speaking Latino students.

English learners need to be evaluated with appropriate English language development assessments. Unfortunately, the information you receive from your district or state usually includes English learners in demographic group results by ethnicity, gender, or poverty. Therefore, you will need to establish a process for regrouping these demographic groups without English learners.

■ School-Level Determination of Differences Between Groups

School-site faculty and administrators typically do not have access to the more sophisticated software and methodologies of running statistical tests to determine significant differences or effect sizes between demographic groups. Therefore, the guidelines we presented in Chapter 3 assist in the determination of whether there are differences between demographic groups. The use of statistical tests and effect sizes is recommended at the district level for staff that have access to student data and knowledge of statistics and statistical software. School-site staff must use student data that are readily available and familiar to teachers and parents.

■ Examples of Student Data Sources

Several types of information are available for you to use in analyzing the performance of demographic groups of students in your schools. Data readily available to most educators include standards-based measures, norm-referenced tests, and educational access measures. The section that follows presents a brief review of each type of data.

Standards-Based Assessments

Standards-based tests are one of the best measures to use in evaluating student academic achievement. These measures are almost universally available in the United States because of the federal requirements of the No Child Left Behind Act or similar state-level requirements. Standards-based tests also include many high school exit exams and various criterion-referenced monitoring tests used by schools. On standards-based tests, students are assessed on what they have learned based on predefined learning outcomes or standards. Standards-based assessments usually provide two scores, scaled scores and performance level scores. Scaled scores usually have a large score range (e.g., scores on the California standards-based test range from 1 to 600) and are used to define student performance levels. Performance levels typically consist of four or five levels that describe student performance in relation to the mastery of the standards. As an example, performance levels may be described as advanced, proficient, basic, below basic, and far below basic levels.

The use of performance levels is recommended at the school-site level because of their availability to the classroom teacher. Scaled scores are recommended for more advanced statistical tests because they are more sensitive to individual differences due to their larger range of scores.

Norm-Referenced Tests

Norm-referenced tests, which compare individual or group scores to a national group norm, are still used in many states, districts, and schools. A norm-referenced test generally answers the question, "How does an individual or group compare to students nationwide who took this test?" This is in contrast to a standards-based test score that indicates the extent of mastery a student has achieved against selected predetermined standards.

Norm-referenced tests, such as the Stanford Achievement Test, California Achievement Test, and Iowa Test of Basic Skills, among others, provide scores available for interpretation. In these tests student achievement is represented as percentile scores, scaled scores, normal curve equivalent (NCE) scores, stanines, and grade equivalents. Two of these scores, scaled scores and NCEs, are based on an equal interval scale and, therefore, are best to use in comparing group performance. Both scores can be converted to percentile scores to assist in interpreting test scores.

Educational Access Measures

Culturally proficient educators realize that student performance is not assessed only through the use of varied tests. These educators fully recognize that there are other measures that, when used properly, shed important light on how the school can affect students in ways that analyzing student test data will never reveal. We offer for your consideration numerous other measures you can and should use to analyze performance gaps between groups of students. We highly recommend that you use these or other measures as part of a comprehensive analysis of student performance. Rightfully, many educators, authors, and policymakers (Bracey, 2000; Kohn, 1998; Kozol, 2005; Wartell & Huelskamp, 1991) have criticized the validity of using single tests and *tests* in general as the sole determiner of the effectiveness of student learning.

Behavioral indicators provide additional important information about students in your school. Systematically gathering and arraying these data will provide you with not only information about your students but rich sources of information so that you and your colleagues will also learn about the culture of your grade level, your department, and your school. Any time you collect information about your students, you are also collecting information about your school. In the space that follows, we describe several types of data to gather. Included with each indicator are suggestions on how these can be measured. As you will notice, some of these indicators are direct measures of student performance, and others are correlated with student achievement.

We note that some of these indicators are easier to access than others. You may want to inquire about how the following indicators are collected and sorted and who tracks such data. Is it someone in your school? Your central office? Both?

Student Attendance. For ease and accuracy of comparison, we recommend that student attendance be defined as the percent of days students attended school. This is especially relevant for schools with high mobility rates so as not to assume that all students are enrolled for the entire school year. This method necessitates collecting two pieces of information—the number of days each student was enrolled during the school year, and the number of days each student attended school. Dividing the number of days the student attended school (numerator) by the number of days the student was enrolled (denominator) provides the percent of days the student attended school. For example, if a school year is 180 days, then a student who is absent for 15 would have an absence ratio of 0.083 (i.e., 15/180). This student was absent for 8.3% of the school year.

Student Suspensions. There are many ways to collect student suspension information. We recommend recording the number of days students are suspended. This information is usually available from the principal or the principal's designee. Days students are suspended translate directly to lost instructional time in the classroom and, thereby, affect student achievement.

Student Dropout and Expulsion Rates. Dropout and expulsion rates are severe indicators of student failure in our school system. These are typically low-incidence occurrences that are required to be reported by the No Child Left Behind Act. This information should, therefore, be available from your school district for your school site.

Student Enrollment in Special Programs. Numerous programs and classes in our schools demonstrate a disproportionate number of student demographic group enrollments. Programs or classes typically found in schools are

- remedial programs,
- special education programs,
- Gifted and Talented programs,
- Honors and Advanced Placement courses, and
- Advancement Via Individual Determination (AVID) and International Baccalaureate (IB) programs.

Determining enrollment patterns in these programs requires that you identify the programs you wish to review and then identify students who participate in the programs.

Additional High School Indicators. Unique indicators exist at the high school level for monitoring student academic progress. These data are related to meeting high school graduation requirements and preparation for college entrance. Data related to high school graduation are as follows:

- Enrollment and successful completion of Algebra 1. This can also be used as an indicator at eighth grade. High school information on Algebra 1 is typically collected at the end of ninth grade because completion at this grade level is a prerequisite to other high school courses.

- Accumulation of high school credits. Again, the number of credits earned is grade specific and can be used to determine whether students are on track to graduate. Recording the number of credits earned at the end of the year for each student by grade level will provide this information.
- Percent of students receiving D, F, or Incomplete grade distributions. Students receiving grades of D, F, and Incomplete are at risk of not graduating from high school. Retrieving this information from school records may be complicated, or the information may not be readily available; however, if available it provides a profile of student success in your school and the likelihood that cultural groups will meet their graduation requirements. As a first step, we suggest that you select one semester and calculate who has received D, F, or Incomplete grades.
- Graduation rates. Graduation rates are determined for each senior class at the end of the students' senior year. These rates can be computed in a variety of ways, including a four-year projection based on ninth-grade enrollment or one-year graduation rates of enrolled seniors. Whichever method you use, you will need to record whether or not a senior student graduated from high school at the end of his or her senior year.
- College preparation and entrance indicators. Indicators related to student college entrance include enrollment in college preparation and Advanced Placement classes. Again, this information can be complicated to collect so we recommend that you use the format established in your district. College preparation class enrollment is typically measured after the completion of the senior year. You can measure enrollment in Advanced Placement classes after the senior year or during a one or two semester block of time. Traditional measures such as SAT and ACT scores can be used to provide additional information about student readiness for college.
- Postgraduate surveys. Surveys of recent graduates can provide information to identify work, education, military, and apprenticeships experiences. In addition to providing a profile of experiences, the survey can elicit respondents' views of areas of strength and suggestions for improvement of high school programs.

Summary of Data Collection Process

The journey to understanding educational access and opportunities for your students begins as you and your colleagues gather and analyze these kinds of data about your student demographic groups. You can use these data as a baseline by which you will be able to judge your educational progress and make needed changes. Perhaps most important, in collecting and analyzing these data you and your colleagues will come together as a professional community; have important discussions about the progress of your students and what you can do to improve access, learning, and achievement for all groups; and, begin to narrow and close gaps that matter.

■ Initial Steps in the Data Collection Process

1. Identify the demographic groups you wish to study at your school. It is best that you have at least 30 students in a demographic group to make a meaningful comparison. This qualifies as enough students to identify a valid and reliable student demographic group and to protect student confidentiality.

2. Make a list of the demographic groups you are going to compare.

3. Identify and make a list of the student information you wish to collect for your analysis of demographic group performance at your school.

4. Identify the source of the information you wish to collect. How do you go about getting the information? Where is the information collected and maintained? At the school site? The central office?

5. Define the data you will be entering. Are you using performance levels for standards-based assessments? NCE scores for norm-referenced tests? Percentages?

6. Determine the best approach for you to collect student information. Information can be collected by hand or electronically in a spreadsheet or database.

■ Reflections on Your Data Collection Process

Which student demographic groups will be studied? Include approximate size of each group. Why are you selecting this particular group?

_____

_____

_____

_____

What is the difference between data and data collecting to indicate student performance, student improvement, and student achievement gaps?

_____

_____

_____

_____

Why is using the peer group model approach important? What important data does it provide when you are trying to measure educational gaps?

_____

_____

_____

_____

What kinds of data beyond achievement test data provide important information about students' progress?

_____

_____

_____

_____

What are you discovering about who has access to student achievement data?

_____

_____

_____

_____

How does this chapter inform your work?

_____

_____

_____

_____

This chapter focused on student-centered data available at your school. These data and the conversations you will have with your colleagues about your findings will provide you with rich information about which groups of students are being well served by your programs and practices. Similarly, these data and the resultant conversations with your colleagues will draw attention to those students not being well served by current programs and practices.

5

Planning the Cultural Proficiency Inquiry

Scientific truth is marvelous, but moral truth is divine and whoever breathes its air and walks by its light has found the lost paradise.

—Horace Mann (2006)

Getting Centered

What compels you to conduct a cultural proficiency inquiry to examine your progress toward serving all demographic groups? Do you have hypotheses of what your inquiry might reveal? What kind of support can you garner for this investigation process?

What questions do you have? What challenges might you and your colleagues face?

_____

_____

_____

_____

The inquiry process is a fact-finding mission. Insofar as facts uncover policies and practices that are barriers to the educational success for some students, we can be compelled to rectify them. To that end, the cultural proficiency inquiry process is not a tool to tell us *how* to close access, learning, and achievement gaps. Rather, the process teaches us how to identify achievement and access gaps, how to project a desired state, and how to begin honest and insightful discussions that may lead to bold actions to better meet the needs of underserved populations.

Inquiry denotes the gathering of facts in order to understand a particular phenomenon. Cultural proficiency inquiry is designed to guide you in learning about your school as a system to determine the extent to which major program components are serving the needs of all student demographic groups. This chapter

- provides a rationale and purpose for your cultural proficiency inquiry,
- identifies major program components (i.e., subsystems within your school) that can be used as leverage points for desired changes, and
- describes steps for conducting the inquiry.

As you read this chapter, think about a particular part of the school system for your inquiry. Are you conducting an inquiry about practices in your classroom? Grade level? Department? Program? School? District? Once you determine the part of the school system to study, we recommend that you stay focused in looking at data only about that part of the school system you are studying.

Rationale for a Cultural Proficiency Inquiry

Numerous self-review processes are available to guide educators and interested community members in analyzing the effectiveness of their educational programs. Most educators have experience with self-reviews to examine program effectiveness related to school improvement, accreditation, or other kinds of program compliance. Similarly, the cultural proficiency inquiry is a self-review process for you to conduct a systematic check of the effectiveness of your programs and practices to better meet the needs of underserved populations.

Distinctive assumptions underlie a cultural proficiency inquiry and differentiate it from other self-review processes. The basic assumptions of a cultural proficiency inquiry are the following:

- not all demographic groups of students are being served well by current programs and practices;
- current educational practices correlate with, if not cause, conditions that meet the needs of some demographic groups of students better than others;
- current resources within the system (i.e., time, people, money, and materials) are not being allocated in ways that ensure equitable outcomes for all students;
- it is possible to remove barriers and reallocate resources so that the needs of all are met by the resources at hand; and
- not everybody in the system is aware of the barriers, equity gaps, and resource misallocations; and, if they are all aware, not everyone is willing to do what it takes to realign the system to be inclusive of the educational needs of underperforming students.

A cultural proficiency inquiry assumes that by examining data, bringing issues to the surface, and provoking discussions, leaders can build knowledge and capacity while also engendering the will for narrowing and closing the gaps that matter in order to unfold the democracy of schooling in the United States, so that the needs of all students are met equally well.

The Purpose of a Cultural Proficiency Inquiry

The primary purposes of a cultural proficiency inquiry are

- to assist users of the inquiry to examine formal and informal data to inform their assumptions and hypothesis about who is and who is not being served,
- to examine the extent to which various parts of the system or the whole system are conducting their functions to meet the needs of underserved populations, and
- to inform the users of the inquiry process about what equity is and what it looks like in practice.

In summary, the inquiry process is a tool to help users conduct investigations about the effectiveness of their program to meet the needs of all student groups, and in so doing come to know what is the current state, what is the desired state, and how far is the gap to get from one to the other.

Program Components to Use as Leverage Points for Change

Districts, schools, and classrooms are organizations that comprise many components or subsystems that can yield data about the overall cultural proficiency of the specific and entire organization. These subsystems are aspects or functions of work that already exist within an educational organization and are critical to its operation. Subsystems in school districts, schools, and classrooms

- adopt or develop specified curriculum and instructional approaches,
- engage in various forms of parent outreach and communication,
- engage in professional development,
- use various forms of assessments, and
- recruit and retain educators.

We also refer to these subsystems as leverage points because these functions have wide-reaching effects on the entire system, and by pressing for change within that particular subsystem, you may get residual change across the system. Working with existing subsystems or leverage points gives you bigger bang for your buck, so to speak. Although there may be many such subsystems or leverage points, in this book we focus on four subsystems as leverage points for creating change in a district, school, or classroom:

- curriculum and instruction,
- assessment and accountability,
- parent and community communication and outreach, and
- professional development.

For these leverage points we have created four rubrics describing the interrelationship of the cultural proficiency continuum and specific aspects of a particular leverage point that already exists within your school. By focusing on one or two leverage points for your inquiry, you target specific functions within your district, school, or classroom for which you may want to create change. When focusing on three or more leverage points, you will have information about many functions across your organization and the foundation for broader, system-wide change.

If you were to examine data simultaneously about the culturally proficient practices within curriculum and instruction, parent outreach and communication, and assessment and accountability, chances are that you would have enough data to make substantial change in your organization. The scope of your inquiry can be as narrowly or broadly focused as you deem appropriate on the basis of your intent, your capacity, and the resources required to facilitate the inquiry process.

Chapters 3 and 4 described multiple entry points to begin to examine gaps between and among student demographic groups. You may already be aware of some of those gaps, or you may want to begin your inquiry without specific knowledge of gaps in order to examine your system overall without predetermined assumptions to see where there is greatest need.

The cultural proficiency inquiry is designed to give you important information about your organizational system (e.g., district, school or classroom, grade level, department, program, etc.). The inquiry is not to provide information about discrete situations, conditions, or occurrences within them such as unequal distribution of textbooks, disparities in attendance at back-to-school nights, or uneven participation in professional development. However, discrete findings such as these certainly play into the bigger picture and may become part of actions designed to address achievement gaps.

We encourage the pioneers among you to identify subsystems and leverage points beyond those identified here and, in collaborative fashion, craft rubrics like the ones we provide in the next chapter. By so doing, you will experience professionally rich conversations and deepened understanding of cultural proficiency.

To guide you through the cultural proficiency inquiry process, we have provided rubrics for the four leverage points we have identified—curriculum and instruction, assessment and accountability, professional development, and parent outreach and communication. These rubrics are derived from the cultural proficiency continuum and the five essential elements of cultural competence we described in Chapter 2. The rubrics are presented in Chapter 6, along with an explanation of how they were constructed and how to use them.

A foundational understanding of the continuum and the essential elements is necessary to effectively use the rubrics presented in Chapter 6. The degree of accuracy in using the rubrics is also related to participants' understanding of the guiding principles and the barriers to cultural proficiency and the ways these barriers manifest across the system. If you want to refresh your knowledge of the four tools of cultural proficiency, please refer to Chapter 2.

We ask you not to view the cultural proficiency inquiry as new work but rather as ongoing work of collecting data about program effectiveness through a new lens, the lens of cultural proficiency, the lens of maximizing service to demographic groups whose needs have been historically minimized and ignored.

Steps for Conducting the Cultural Proficiency Inquiry

Before reviewing the specific steps of the inquiry process, note that although we propose a sequence to the steps, it matters not whether you begin with defining the scope, identifying the participants, or designing the process for the inquiry. Internal and external forces for change may have you starting at any one of these points and working back and forth within these steps as you get more information, interest, and buy-in and as you clarify the vision for the inquiry. So although it is not as important to begin your inquiry steps as outlined here, it is critical to base your inquiry on some existing assumptions or conclusions evinced by current data or data patterns. Likewise, it is not essential to answer every question posed for each step. Instead, you should answer the "essential question(s)" posed. The "questions for consideration" can be used to guide your response to the essential question. You may encounter the same or similar questions at different steps of the inquiry process. The questions are to guide, not constrict, your inquiry process. Be creative and flexible with this process to meet the needs of those involved in the inquiry.

A cultural proficiency inquiry consists of seven steps. The first five steps are the "pre-work" necessary to have an effective data collection, analysis, and reporting experience. Thoughtful consideration of the first five steps on the cultural proficiency inquiry sets the stage for meaningful dialogue among members of the inquiry study team. Once the inquiry team has made the decisions inherent to the first five steps, consideration of the data becomes a team effort.

The pre-work:

1. Define the context.

2. Establish the purpose for the inquiry.

3. Define the scope of the inquiry.

4. Identify and select participants to conduct the inquiry.

5. Design the process to conduct the inquiry.

Then, the data:

1. Collect and analyze data gleaned from the inquiry.

2. Interpret data and report findings.

The section that follows outlines each of the steps or tasks for the inquiry process. Questions for reflection and discussion are provided to guide you through each task in the inquiry process.

■ Step 1: Define the Context for the Inquiry

Essential Questions:

What is your organizational unit of study (i.e., district, school classroom, grade level, department, program)? Which leverage points will be the focus of your cultural proficiency inquiry (i.e., curriculum and instruction, assessment and accountability, parent outreach and communication, or professional development)?

_____

_____

_____

_____

Questions for Consideration:

1. What general or specific condition(s), situation(s), or problem(s) related to gaps for your students give impetus to this inquiry? Which students are you concerned about?

2. How have you come to be aware of the problem? What other stakeholders are aware of the problem? How have they become aware?

3. Why are you focusing on this particular organizational unit for your inquiry?

4. Why are you using this/these leverage points and cultural proficiency rubrics to guide your inquiry?

5. Other information to inform the context of your inquiry . . .

■ Step 2: Establish the Purpose for the Inquiry Study

Essential Questions:

What is the purpose of this inquiry? What do you hope to see happen as a result of this inquiry?

_____

_____

_____

_____

Questions for Consideration:

1. What data already exist that point to one or more educational gaps that you want to close? Why does this particular problem concern you?

2. Which groups are you studying? Are your data in aggregated or disaggregated form? Should you disaggregate the data further for groups within groups?

3. What additional data would you like to have that you don't have now? How would having these data clarify your purpose?

4. Do the data indicate a new or ongoing pattern? Describe the pattern.

5. Why will inquiry into this or these particular leverage point(s) help you close the gap you noted in question 1 above?

6. Other information to inform the context of your inquiry . . .

■ Step 3: Define the Scope of the Inquiry

Essential Questions:

What is the scope of this inquiry? How many leverage points will you examine at what organizational units? What resources will you need to allocate to the inquiry? (Remember that resources are time, people, materials, and money.)

_____

_____

_____

_____

Questions to Consider:

1. How much time will you allocate to this inquiry from starting point to analysis and reporting of findings? How much time can you allocate from the current schedule, and what additional time will you need to create? How much time will you allocate for

   - Start-up and organization?
   - Orientation and training?
   - Data collection?
   - Data sharing and analysis?
   - Writing report of findings?
   - Disseminating report findings (to whom)?

2. How many stakeholders will participate, from what representative groups, and what role(s) will they play?

3. What materials, equipment, and provisions will you need to gather for you and for other participants of the inquiry? Will you need to hire consultants? For technical assistance? For training?

4. Will there be costs for travel, mileage, reprographics, secretarial support, and compensation or substitute coverage?

5. What financial resources can you access for your needs? What financial resources do you need to acquire or develop?

6. Other information to inform the context of your inquiry . . .

■ Step 4: Identify and Select Inquiry Participants

Essential Question:

How will you identify and fairly select participants to be involved in the inquiry?

_____

_____

_____

_____

Questions to Consider:

1. What groups will be represented? Will they be staff, volunteers, or applicants selected by a process?

2. What roles will participants play?

3. How will you ensure representation from appropriate cultural, gender, professional, experiential, geographic, age, and interest groups? How will you integrate into your participant group those members from present and past committees who have important knowledge, expertise, or perspectives about the issues you will be examining?

4. How will you ensure that meeting times are convenient or equally inconvenient for all participants?

5. How will you educate all participants about cultural proficiency, the data, the issues under investigation, and the process of this inquiry?

6. Other information to inform the identification and selection of your inquiry . . .

■ Step 5: Design the Process for the Inquiry

Essential Question:

Given the purpose, scope, and timeline you identified above, how will you plan to implement your cultural proficiency inquiry?

_____

_____

_____

_____

Steps to Consider:

1. Develop sample agenda for the following activities and meetings:
   - Plan to communicate your plan to key leaders to get support for it
   - Plan for identifying and selecting participants
   - Orientation meetings for participants of the inquiry
   - Training sessions (by topic, by date)
   - Data collection sessions
   - Data analysis and sharing meetings
   - Reporting and disseminating findings and next steps

2. What experts will you need to assist you both inside of and outside of your organizational unit? What experts or consultants will you call on to help present information about data to multiple stakeholders in clear and concise ways?

3. What material resources do you have? What material resources do you need?

4. Other information to inform the design of your inquiry process . . .

■ Step 6: Collect and Analyze Data (Part III of this book guides the data collection process)

Essential Questions:

What data will participants collect and analyze? What data do participants have access to (formal or informal)? What important data do participants not have, and need? How can you facilitate securing or disseminating these data? Who will monitor the process so that the data collection, analysis, interpretation, and reporting yield accurate information?

_____

_____

_____

_____

Questions to Consider:

1. What data and data sources (formal and informal) will best inform the inquiry about this leverage point for your organization?

2. What data are readily available about the gaps you are studying, within the leverage point(s) you are studying, for your particular organizational unit?

3. What data are not available but needed? How will you get them and in what format will you present them to the participants of the inquiry?

4. Who will help you manage this step in the process so that the data are easy to understand by all stakeholders? How will you structure sessions and meetings to discuss data?

5. Other information to inform your data collection and analysis . . .

■ Step 7: Interpret and Report Results

Essential Questions:

To what extent did your cultural proficiency inquiry meet the purpose(s) you identified in Step 2? What did you learn that you wanted to learn? What else did you learn in this process? Where might you go from here?

_____

_____

_____

_____

Questions to Consider:

1. What are some of the essential findings or conclusions of your inquiry?

2. What patterns or correlations emerged?

3. Which of your hypotheses were confirmed by your inquiry? What unanticipated findings emerged?

4. By using the specific leverage point rubrics you selected, what did you learn about your progress toward cultural proficiency?

5. One of the most important questions we can ask is "now that we have the data, so what?" The "so what" question is fundamental to making the data useful for improving student learning.

6. Considering this cultural proficiency inquiry process and its results, what might be some next steps for your district, school, classroom, or program?

7. Who needs to be informed about the results of this inquiry process, and how will you inform them?

8. Other questions to inform interpreting your results and reporting on your findings . . .

Cultural proficiency inquiry and the discussions, processes, and findings associated with it have given you a treasure chest of information about how well your organization is meeting the needs of your student demographic groups. Used carefully, the leverage point rubrics will have given you important diagnostic information about the current strengths and needs of the subsystems you examined while at the same time describing desired outcomes and projecting next steps for you to attain them.

Although this work is complex and difficult, it must be done. It is our *moral imperative* in a democracy. Data collection and analysis is critical to raising people's awareness that we are not serving some of our student groups, in spite of our good intentions. Without the data, we can get caught in the "opinion quicksand" and "blame game" and never get on with the business of realigning systems and subsystems so that all students receive the educational opportunities promised to them by our founding fathers.

This book, and particularly this chapter, has provided you with a process and tools to sharpen your skills for organizing and leading the work. Skill alone will not get us to the finish line if we do not have the will to stay the course and finish what we start. The will comes from our sense of urgency and responsibility to follow the words of Horace Mann (2006), "to make Education then, beyond all other devices of human origin, the great equalizer of the conditions of men, the balance-wheel of the social machinery." Skill, will, and action together are the manifestations of advocacy, the critical component of our work that constitutes Chapters 7–10.

6

Rubrics as Keys to the Cultural Proficiency Inquiry

The truth is that our finest moments are most likely to occur when we are feeling deeply uncomfortable, unhappy, or unfulfilled. For it is only in such moments, propelled by our discomfort, that we are likely to step out of our ruts and start searching for different ways or truer answers.

—M. Scott Peck (2000)

Getting Centered

How would you measure cultural proficiency in society? How would you measure it in schools and classrooms? How would you teach someone to become a more culturally competent educator? How can cultural proficiency help us close educational and achievement gaps?

_____

_____

_____

_____

One of the disquieting features of many school reform efforts is the too often narrow focus on test scores and the admonition to close achievement gaps. Test scores may have very little to do with achievement gaps. Test scores certainly do not cause achievement gaps, although the best example of achievement gaps can be seen when students take a standardized test and we report the results. What if we could quantify and test student wellness and readiness to start school? What if we could quantify and test the ways in which some students and their parents get access to the best educational resources while others are left behind? What if we could quantify and test the quality of student-teacher interaction and classroom opportunities to learn for African American, Latino, and First Nations children?

Achievement gaps have nothing to do with test scores and everything to do with the way some students are educated. If we could measure the latter, we could realign our efforts so that the gaps on standardized test scores are not so wide between student demographic groups. But either because we have not the skill to do so, nor the will, often we do nothing. We wait until achievement test results show glaring disparities between demographic groups of children, and because we assume we have been giving all students the same *opportunities* to learn, we arrive at the conclusion that their underperformance on standardized tests is *their* fault. We blame them, their parents, their homes, their communities, but we do not blame our blindness to the gaps from the beginning, and we do not wonder whether we have educated these students or *miseducated* them into the achievement gap (Education Trust, 2006).

By the time the gaps manifest in achievement scores, a too often heard lament is that "it is too late, or too difficult for us to even try." By the time many students take their first standardized test, the pattern has been set. The gaps, long since established, manifest now in the test scores, and suddenly we have something called the achievement gap. However, we hold that *test scores serve as an indicator of how successful we, the educators, are in our professional practices.*

This chapter presents a set of four rubrics that help us measure education gaps for our students, and if we are willing to change our practices, or course of action, we can narrow and close the insidious achievement gap because we will have closed the many practitioner gaps that feed it.

The rubrics provide concrete examples of what stasis or change looks like at various stages along the continuum to cultural proficiency, and are a fundamental component of the cultural proficiency inquiry process. The rubrics provoke users to mediate their own learning (i.e., change) as well as the learning of colleagues as they see new ways to interact with and educate students who are different from them.

The goal of cultural proficiency inquiry is viewing change as an "inside-out" process in which one becomes aware of unintended or unconscious decisions, actions, and attitudes that impede the learning of children and youth, and then systematically dismantle the barriers, replacing them with culturally proficient policies, practices, and behaviors. The rubrics are the keys to unlocking our ignorance and opening our minds to possibilities for educating students with whom we have not been successful.

Why the Cultural Proficiency Inquiry Process for Closing Equity Gaps?

The heightened focus on the achievement gap and the need to make drastic school improvement at breakneck speed have led to low-income children and children of color being thrust into learning environments where the predominant focus is on one-size-fits-all curriculum and pacing plans that are supposed to improve test scores, even if they do not improve learning. Little support is offered to help teachers scaffold learning for students whose prerequisite skills and knowledge are inadequate to meet the demands of higher standards and rigid instructional approaches. Children, especially those who need the most help in school, are falling through the cracks in droves. Educational triage teams are arriving on the scene to conduct program reviews and audits, leaving behind a trail of recommendations for already beleaguered schools to implement. We don't argue against such practices as a possible beginning point, but we are concerned that these practices are becoming institutionalized and lead to a climate of mistrust, fear, anger, and, most important, a continued ignoring of the complex needs of our children and youth.

We devised the cultural proficiency inquiry approach as an alternative to externally imposed audits and reviews. Cultural proficiency inquiry provides educators with a self-review process and rubrics to examine why and how some students are not being educated to their full potential. With data from the self-review process, educators can make small and big changes to begin to narrow and close the many gaps experienced by too many of our children that lead to the test-score or achievement gap. When the achievement gap is framed as an educational opportunity equity gap, responsibility moves from testing students to determining if they are failing or succeeding to using test scores as one indicator that leads us to examine *our* practices as teachers, counselors, and administrators. With external reviews we often ask, "Why are students underperforming?" The cultural proficiency inquiry provokes us to ask, "In what ways are we underserving our students who need the most?"

The four rubrics that we have developed to aid in this equity self-review or inquiry process help examine our practices within the areas of curriculum and instruction, assessment and accountability, parent and community communication and outreach, and professional development.

Keys to Change

For the past decade or so school reformers have discussed school change in terms of leverage points for change (DuFour, DuFour, Eaker, & Karhanek, 2004; DuFour, Eaker, & DuFour, 2005; Fullan, 2003; Kegan, 2001; Reeves, 2000; Senge et al., 1999, 2000). Leverage points are the policies and practices over which educators have the most direct impact. As we discussed above and in Chapter 5, prominent leverage points for changing school practices are curriculum, instruction, assessment and accountability practices, processes for communicating with parents, and professional development. Each of these leverage points provides educators with specific opportunities to shape important function within their organizations as well as the education of our students.

Change in schools can be either *reformative* or *transformative.* Often, reform initiatives driven by external forces (e.g., No Child Left Behind) result in change processes that are compliance driven. Challenging one's own assumptions about who is being served by our schools, on the other hand, drives deeper, transformative initiatives

(Argyris, 1990; Fullan, 2003; Hilliard, 1991; Schein, 1989). Educators who examine and challenge their own assumptions are prepared to challenge the system in such a manner that schools can be transformed to serve all students. It is the transformative approach to system change that brings together individual educators' moral commitment to developing schools that well serve all demographic groups of students.

In this chapter we provide examples from our work with P–16 (preschool through postsecondary) educators, organized into matrices and associated tools, to focus on how people transform their practices as administrators, teachers, and counselors in ways that serve the academic and social needs of their students. The four matrices organized into rubrics are curriculum and instruction, assessment and accountability, professional development, and parent and community communications and outreach.

The cultural proficiency inquiry approach provides you with a perspective of policies and practices *in use.* The rubrics provide concrete examples of the assumptions that either facilitate or hinder change, a condition known as "stasis." When educators accurately identify the assumptions that guide their work and combine them with test data, they have guidelines for changing professional values, behavior, policies, and practices in ways that benefit historically underserved learners. Fundamental to personal transformation is learning to mediate one's own learning (i.e., change) as well as the learning of colleagues.

Cultural Proficiency Rubrics

In developing the rubrics, the first step was to operationally define each of the leverage points in the context of each of the essential elements of cultural competence. Table 6.1, "Leverage Points and the Five Essential Elements of Cultural Competence," presents the four leverage points on the horizontal axis—curriculum and instruction, assessment and accountability, parent and community communication and outreach, and professional development—and on the vertical axis are the five essential elements—assessing cultural knowledge, valuing diversity, managing the dynamics of difference, adapting to diversity, and institutionalizing cultural knowledge. The rubrics are available on the CD provided with this book. They are under the subdirectory Rubrics.

Table 6.1 Leverage Points and the Five Essential Elements of Cultural Competence

			Leverage Points		
Five Essential Elements	Curriculum and Instruction	Assessment	Parents and Community	Professional Development
Valuing Diversity	Extent to which curriculum reflects diversity.	Extent to which cultural differences are used to gather data.	Extent to which parent and community diversity is valued.	Extent to which professional development addresses cultural issues.
Assessing Culture	Extent to which curriculum provides opportunities for educators and students to learn about self and others.	Extent to which disaggregated data are used to enhance knowledge and shape practice.	Extent to which community involvement facilitates the identification, assessment, and development of cultural identity.	Extent to which professional development addresses issues of cultural identity.
Managing the Dynamics of Difference	Extent to which curriculum promotes multiple perspectives.	Extent to which data are used to address the gaps between cultural groups.	Extent to which community involvement efforts develop the capacity to mediate cultural conflict between and among diverse parent and community groups and the school.	Extent to which professional development promotes and models the use of inquiry and dialogue related to multiple perspectives and issues arising from diversity.
Adapting to Diversity	Extent to which cultural knowledge is integrated into the curriculum.	Extent to which assessments are changed to meet the needs of cultural groups.	Extent to which people and schools change to meet the needs of the community.	The extent to which professional learning facilitates change to meet the needs of the community.
Institutionalizing	Extent to which values and policies support culturally responsive curriculum.	Extent to which assessment data shape values and policies to meet the needs of cultural groups.	Extent to which people and schools integrate knowledge about diverse community and organizational cultures into daily practice.	The extent to which professional development shapes policies and practices that meet the needs of a diverse community.

Prior to reviewing each of the cultural proficiency rubrics, it is important to note that the descriptions in the cells of the rubrics are to be illustrative and not prescriptive. It is our intent that you use the illustrations from the rubrics to develop your own manner of addressing the topic similar to those provided. Our interest is that you develop acuity in recognizing you and your colleagues frame your conversations about your students.

■ Reflection

In this chapter we are posing the reflection questions prior to presenting the content to guide your reading and study of the rubrics. Use any or all of the reflection questions after you review each rubric to think about your observations and discuss them with colleagues. For ease of reading and writing your reflections, the questions are repeated in appropriate places.

As you review each rubric, what do you see as the main difference between the practices described on the right side of the rubric compared to the practices described on the left side of the rubric?

In the introduction to this chapter, we stated that the cultural proficiency rubrics were the keys to unlocking our unawareness and opening our minds to possibilities for educating students with whom we have not been successful. What possibilities do you see for educating all student demographic groups to high levels that you did not see before?

How might you be able to use this tool in your professional practice?

_____

_____

_____

_____

■ Curriculum and Instruction Rubric

Table 6.2 presents the curriculum and instruction rubric. As you read the descriptions under the "curriculum and instruction" column from Table 6.1, you will notice that the descriptions are imported into the first column of Table 6.2.

How to read Table 6.2, the curriculum and instruction rubric:

- Note the rubric is composed of rows and columns.
- Each of the rows is one of the five standards referred to as an "essential element of cultural competence."

- There are seven columns. At the top of the first column is the title "essential elements." A brief description of the element is given in the context of the curriculum and instruction topic.
- Each of the next six columns is one of the six points of the cultural proficiency continuum.
- The fifth column is titled "cultural competence." Each of the descriptors in that column describes one of the essential elements of cultural competence. The language is in active voice and describes actions that can be taken today in schools.
- The sixth column is titled "cultural proficiency." The description is future focused and measurable.

■ Reflection

What do you see as the main difference between the practices described on the right side of the rubric and the practices described on the left side of the rubric?

In using this cultural proficiency rubric as a key to unlocking our unawareness and opening our minds to possibilities for educating students with whom we have not been successful, what possibilities do you see for educating all student demographic groups to high levels that you did not see before?

How might you be able to use this tool in your professional practice?

_____

_____

_____

_____

■ Assessment and Accountability Rubric

Table 6.3 presents the assessment and accountability rubric. When you read the descriptions under the "assessment" column from Table 6.1, as with the previous matrices you will notice that the descriptions are imported into the first column of Table 6.3. The section that follows the table guides you in how to read the rubric.

Table 6.2 Curriculum and Instruction Rubric

Five Essential Elements	Cultural Destructiveness	Cultural Incapacity	Cultural Blindness	Cultural Precompetence	Cultural Competence	Cultural Proficiency
Assessing Cultural Knowledge Extent to which curriculum provides opportunities for educators and students to learn about self and others.	Limit or prohibit sharing of cultural knowledge and developing cultural identity.	Promote assimilation to the dominant culture and dominant learning styles and language.	Ignore aspects of culture (staff or students) that connect culture and learning.	Recognizing that the curriculum does not include students' cultural perspectives. Incorporate into the curriculum information and resources that may reflect students' perspectives.	Regularly provide opportunities for students to contribute their knowledge and perspectives about a lesson's topic(s) and use the knowledge to plan and sequence the lesson.	Assess the gap between the teacher's culture, the culture of the curriculum, and the culture of the students and seek ongoing opportunities to learn about and use culturally responsive curriculum.
Valuing Diversity Extent to which curriculum reflects diversity.	Select and implement curriculum and use resources that denigrate specific perspectives or groups, and/or provide incomplete or inaccurate portrayals of events, individuals, or groups.	Select and implement curriculum and use resources that reflect dominant group values, perspectives, and language.	Implement curriculum and use resources and languages recommended by state educational agencies and publishers, thereby providing limited cultural perspectives.	Recognize that curriculum may provide limited cultural perspectives. Select and develop supplemental curriculum and resources that provide information about contributions of diverse groups.	Select, develop, and implement curricula that reflect diverse perspectives and languages and provide inclusive, accurate portrayal of historical events and cultural groups.	Promote and develop students' advocacy for social justice.

(Continued)

Table 6.2 (Continued)

Five Essential Elements	Cultural Destructiveness	Cultural Incapacity	Cultural Blindness	Cultural Precompetence	Cultural Competence	Cultural Proficiency
Managing the Dynamics of Difference Extent to which curriculum promotes multiple perspectives.	Ignore, seek, or alter data to validate the placement of students into rigid, limiting curricular paths that provide negative educational consequences for all students.	View the core program as meeting the needs of all students. Underperforming students are tracked into rigid curricular paths judged to be the most effective approach to assimilate and advance students.	Implement only mandated state and federal curriculum and interventions determined to be of maximum benefit to underperforming students.	Recognizing that the curriculum may not be accessible to all students, teachers may differentiate instruction, at times inappropriately providing less challenging lessons for underperforming students.	Provide students curriculum options that are challenging and incorporate inquiry and higher order thinking skills that personalize connections and evoke multiple perspectives. Underperforming students receive ongoing, timely, and personalized support from peers, teachers, and parents.	Provide students opportunities to *learn how to learn*—develop academic ability, intellective competence, and advocacy for social justice.
Adapting to Diversity Extent to which cultural knowledge is integrated into the curriculum.	Select and use curriculum that perpetuates inaccurate and/or negative portrayal of diverse groups and historical events.	Use curriculum that portrays values and behaviors of the dominant group to promote the	Embrace standards, standardized curriculum, resources, textbooks, and standardized tests to ensure equality	Recognizing students' cultural differences, curriculum may be supplemented with information about cultural	Integrate and infuse into existing curriculum culturally relevant content and differentiated instructional	Promote multiple perspectives in the curriculum to model and develop advocacy practices for social justice.

Five Essential Elements	Cultural Destructiveness	Cultural Incapacity	Cultural Blindness	Cultural Precompetence	Cultural Competence	Cultural Proficiency
	Curriculum denigrates culturally different groups and events through omissions, distortions. and fallacious assumptions.	assimilation of diverse groups. Staff believes that assimilation is integral to success.	across the curriculum for all student groups without regard for cultural differences.	contributions or events without integrating such into the curriculum.	approaches/resources to meet the needs of all students.	
Institutionalizing Extent to which values and policies support culturally responsive curriculum.	Create policies and practices that ensure a curriculum that excludes, denigrates, and misrepresents diverse groups and historical events. Actively pursue the identification and elimination of perspectives that threaten the *desired* perspective.	Create policies and practices that protect agency-sanctioned curriculum and instructional approaches while justifying them as beneficial for assimilating culturally different groups.	Standardize agency-sanctioned curriculum and instructional resources to meet the needs of all student groups.	Recognizing the limitation of the existing curriculum to be culturally responsive, staff may integrate culturally responsive approaches and materials.	Create policies and practices to ensure that agency-sanctioned curriculum is enhanced with information, instructional approaches, and resources to maximize the learning of all students. Strategies to ensure student success are articulated vertically and horizontally across grade levels and departments within schools and between feeder schools. Students, staff, and parents regularly collaborate to examine data leading to continuous improvement of the curriculum program.	Enthusiastically embrace a districtwide responsibility for closing learning and achievement gaps.

Table 6.3 Assessment and Accountability

5 Essential Elements	Cultural Destructiveness	Cultural Incapacity	Cultural Blindness	Cultural Precompetence	Cultural Competence	Cultural Proficiency
Assessing Cultural Knowledge Extent to which educators understand the limitations of standardized tests for diverse student populations, make appropriate assessment accommodations, use multiple assessment tools, and use disaggregated data to shape practice to meet their needs.	Intentionally use culturally inappropriate test(s) that reinforce misdiagnosis, misplacement, and invalid perspectives about students' learning outcomes and needs. Avoid or resist collecting data and/or misuse data to disseminate inaccurate conclusions about diverse cultural groups.	Use traditional and unaccommodated assessments and data to sort, select, remediate, and justify the assimilation of culturally diverse groups to the dominant school culture and curriculum.	Unaware that culture impacts student performance on assessment and that tests are culturally biased, use single measures of assessment. Unaware of the need to collect or sort data to learn about the progress and/or needs of culturally diverse groups.	Recognizing the connection between culture and learning, use multiple measures that may begin to reflect student cultural differences. Recognizing limited knowledge about some cultural groups, use disaggregated data but may draw inaccurate conclusions or make decisions that may not meet their needs.	Use multiple measures of assessment that reflect students' cultures and language backgrounds. Collect and use disaggregated data to inform all stakeholders about the progress and needs of culturally diverse groups	Advocate for selecting and designing assessment tools that reflect the diversity of students. Advocate for collecting and using disaggregated data to analyze demographic trends and anticipate the needs of ever-changing student populations while closing gaps for current population.
Valuing Diversity Extent to which educators value the culture and languages of students in the assessment process, thus ensuring assessment	Avoid, resist, or provoke dissent for making assessment accommodations that meet diverse student needs. Avoid or resist collecting or disaggregating data that reflect	Believe that student cultural and language differences are deficits and use single assessments and test scores to determine student learning and placement in programs.	Aware of differences in achievement between groups but believe that standardized tests and traditional assessments are valid and reflect the status quo.	Recognize student cultural diversity may lead to initial inquiry about multiple measures or assessment accommodations. Recognizing limitation of information from	Believing that all students can meet high standards, seek opportunities to learn about students' cultures and languages. Commit to using valid and reliable	Sustain a community culture that advocates for high standards for underserved students, and solicits community input about the cultural, linguistic, and learning patterns of all students.

5 Essential Elements	Cultural Destructiveness	Cultural Incapacity	Cultural Blindness	Cultural Precompetence	Cultural Competence	Cultural Proficiency
methods that are valid and reliable for diverse student populations, and believe that all students can meet classroom and state standards and expectations.	cultural differences in the community. Use data to eliminate or restrict programs and services for specific cultural groups.	Use disaggregated data to justify test deficits among demographic groups and to maintain programs and services that support the status quo.	Use aggregate data to promote homogeneity and justify common approaches.	singular data sources, educators collect and analyze data from multiple sources, and begin to learn which may be invalid, unreliable, cumbersome or inconclusive.	assessment for diverse student groups and to educating parents and students about the purposes and uses of assessments. Collect and use disaggregated data from multiple sources to develop an accurate picture of student achievement.	Inform all stakeholders about the appropriate uses of assessment, advocate for reliable, valid assessment measures, and share multiple sources of data to inform and support the progress of all students.
Managing the Dynamics of Difference Extent to which educators and parents collaborate to ensure that assessment produces valid results for diverse learners and does not lead to negative educational and life-consequences	Avoid, resist, or provoke dissent for information that would lead to different methods of assessment for underserved students. Use data about achievement gaps of demographic student groups to justify their deficit status and unworthiness of resources.	Believing that traditional, singular assessments and standardized tests lead to accurate information about students' progress, resist seeking additional or alternative information about students Use data about learning and achievement gaps	Since differences between groups are expected, there is no need to seek further information about cultural issues that could influence student performance and assessment. Minimize collecting, disaggregating, and analyzing data that provide	Recognizing that learning and achievement gaps exist between demographic groups, educators begin to seek input about the implications of culture on assessment. Assessment practices and accommodations may be superficial or applied across	Collaborate with other stakeholders to develop and use reliable and valid assessments that support student learning and are used to make decisions about student progress. Use learning and achievement gap data to provoke ongoing inquiry, investigation, and decisions to meet	Advocate for authentic partnerships and collaboration that lead to assessment methods and tools that reflect the cultural and linguistic assets of diverse student groups. Use learning and achievement gap data to initiate actions that narrow and close

(Continued)

Table 6.3 (Continued)

5 Essential Elements	Cultural Destructiveness	Cultural Incapacity	Cultural Blindness	Cultural Precompetence	Cultural Competence	Cultural Proficiency
for students; seek cultural understanding about students in order to bridge learning gaps and use data to shape conversations and understanding about student needs and educational gaps.		to promote deficit thinking about underperforming demographic groups, leading to decisions that serve to widen the gaps between them.	information about the status, needs, and gaps between cultural groups due to discomfort in noticing difference and a belief in a prevailing meritocracy.	the board to all demographic student groups, and risk making inaccurate or unreliable conclusions about student needs and gaps.	the needs of diverse student groups.	learning and achievement gaps for students while also addressing and removing the systemic barriers that contribute to gaps.
Adapting to Diversity Extent to which educators adapt or change practices based on knowledge of students' cultures and languages and promote assessment practices and decisions that help students rather than hinder their progress; and use data to shape	Avoid, resist, or provoke dissent for any accommodations to assessment practices for diverse student groups; dispute that diverse groups have special learning and assessment needs. Use assessment data to avoid, resist, sabotage, and provoke dissent against	Believe that traditional, singular assessments and standardized tests lead to accurate information about students' progress and therefore avoid making any accommodations to formal and informal assessments. Use assessment data to justify the status quo and for	Use assessments and data to diagnose the learning progress of all students without consideration of cultural or linguistic differences.	Recognizing that assessments do not adequately or accurately measure some students' learning or potential, make superficial or generic adaptations that may not meet learning needs of some demographic groups. Use incomplete data to make	Change classroom assessment practices to reflect students' cultures and languages while maintaining rigorous content. Use assessment data to make decisions and adaptations to improve learning and achievement for all demographic groups.	Advocate for formal and informal assessments that meet the needs of diverse students. Create a data-driven culture ensuring that all stakeholders collect, disaggregate, and analyze data from multiple sources to examine progress of all cultural groups.

5 Essential Elements	Cultural Destructiveness	Cultural Incapacity	Cultural Blindness	Cultural Precompetence	Cultural Competence	Cultural Proficiency
practice to meet the needs of demographic groups and close learning and achievement gaps.	adaptations to better meet the needs of some cultural groups.	remediating students rather than examining systemwide barriers to learning and achievement.		programmatic adaptations that may not meet the needs of demographic groups or narrow and close gaps.		Develop plans and initiate actions to make systemwide changes to meet learning needs and close gaps between all demographic groups.
Institutionalizing Cultural Knowledge Extent to which everyone in the school community demonstrates a culture of advocacy for underserved students and a commitment to monitoring the extent to which access, learning, and achievement gaps are being narrowed and closed; use assessment data to determine the needs of all demographic groups and develop strategies to close learning and achievement gaps.	Promote and develop policies, practices, and structures across the system that ensure one-size-fits-all assessments, resulting in data which does not provide valid, reliable information about all students' progress and needs. Use data to make decisions that limit or deny resources to meet the needs of all demographic groups.	Maintain policies, practices, and structures that impose one-size-fits-all assessments across the system that do not adequately measure progress for diverse student groups. Use data from such assessments to reinforce deficit perceptions about student potential and make decisions that have negative educational consequences for diverse student groups.	Policies, practices, and structures rely on the adequacy of current state and district assessment systems to provide adequate information about the needs and progress of all student groups. This limits the capacity to use assessment alternatives that better meet the needs of diverse student groups and to close learning and achievement gaps.	Recognizing that traditional or standardized assessments and test assessments do not adequately measure all students' learning, begin to learn about accommodations or assessment alternatives that provide valid or reliable data-informed decisions for diverse student groups.	Systemwide structure and resources allow educators to collaborate on assessment strategies effective with diverse student groups, analyze student work, create common rubrics, and deepen their assessment literacy and improve learning for underserved demographic groups.	Advocate for policies, practices, and structures at the district and state levels that ensure assessment alternatives, accommodations, and accountability systems are valid, reliable, fair, and equitable for all demographic student groups. The data-driven culture of the school provides ongoing structures and resources for analyzing appropriate school and student data to close learning and achievement gaps.

How to read Table 6.3, the assessment and accountability rubric:

- Note the rubric is composed of rows and columns.
- Each of the rows is one of the five standards referred to as an essential element of cultural competence.
- There are seven columns. At the top of the first column is the title "essential elements." A brief description of the element is given in the context of the assessment and accountability topic.
- Each of the next six columns is one of the six points of the cultural proficiency continuum.
- The fifth column is titled "cultural competence." Each of the descriptors in that column describes one of the essential elements of cultural competence. The language is in active voice and describes actions that can be taken today in schools.
- The sixth column is titled "cultural proficiency." The description is future focused and measurable.

■ Reflection

What do you see as the main difference between the practices described on the right side of the rubric and the practices described on the left side of the rubric?

In using this cultural proficiency rubric as a key to unlocking our unawareness and opening our minds to possibilities for educating students with whom we have not been successful, what possibilities do you see for educating all student demographic groups to high levels that you did not see before?

How might you be able to use this tool in your professional practice?

_____

_____

_____

_____

■ Parent and Community Outreach and Communication Rubric

Table 6.4 presents the parent and community outreach and communication rubric. When you read the descriptions under the "parent and community" column from Table 6.1, once again you will notice that the descriptions are imported into the first column of Table 6.4. The section that follows the table guides you in how to read the rubric.

Table 6.4 Parent and Community Communication and Outreach Rubric

	Cultural Destructiveness	Cultural Incapacity	Cultural Blindness	Cultural Precompetence	Cultural Competence	Cultural Proficiency
Assessing Cultural Knowledge Extent to which community involvement facilitates the identification, assessment, and development of cultural identity.	Ignore, intimidate, or punish the expression of needs of diverse parent and community groups.	Help culturally diverse parent and community members by purposefully assimilating them into the dominant culture.	Parent, community, and school leaders are from select communities without regard to different cultural groups.	Recognizing the importance of knowing about each others' cultures, parent, community, and school leaders may learn about each other in authentic ways.	Parent, community, and school leaders learn about each others' cultures in order to bridge the gaps between and among home, community, and school cultures.	Parent, community, and school leaders continuously scan the environment in order to be responsive to ever-changing community demographics.
Valuing Diversity Extent to which parent and community diversity is valued.	Actively prevent involvement of different cultural groups in making decisions about programs and services that meet the needs of all students.	Identify parents and community members to remediate their cultural deficiencies.	Parent and community involvement responsive to legal mandates without respect to different cultural groups.	Recognizing need to involve culturally diverse community groups in decision making, may include some but not all groups appropriately.	Involve representative constituencies of parents and community members as partners in making decisions about programs and services that meet the needs of all students.	Representative constituencies of parents and community members advocate closing achievement gaps and develop and model advocacy for social justice practices.
Managing the Dynamics of Difference	Sabotage involvement of some parent groups	Ignore parent and community groups that are working to	Facilitate groups working together to find common	Recognizing emerging intergroup conflict, staff	Create a culture that encourages multiple	Staff, parents, and community groups work together to

(Continued)

Table 6.4 (Continued)

	Cultural Destructiveness	Cultural Incapacity	Cultural Blindness	Cultural Precompetence	Cultural Competence	Cultural Proficiency
Extent to which community involvement efforts develop the capacity to mediate cultural conflict between and among diverse parent and community groups and the school.	by instigating competition for scarce resources that results in intergroup conflict.	address issues important to them.	ground on divisive issues.	may develop conflict resolution strategies or identify *key liaisons* within diverse cultural groups.	perspectives and builds capacity for and practices dialogue between and among all community, parent, and school groups.	anticipate the needs of the ever-changing community and associated issues.
Adapting to Diversity Extent to which people and schools change to meet the needs of the community.	Parents and/or school staff prevent changes intended to benefit culturally different community and student groups.	Parents and school staff consider meeting the needs of culturally different groups as divisive.	Parents and school staff do not acknowledge the need to meet the needs of culturally different community groups.	Recognizing differences between home and school cultures, parent, community, and school leaders may begin to address needs of diverse community populations.	Parents and school staff work together to identify and address needs of diverse cultural populations.	Staff, parents, and community work together to meet the needs of all cultural groups and anticipate and plan for changes within the community.
Institutionalizing Extent to which people and schools integrate knowledge about diverse community and organizational cultures into daily practice.	School staff create policies and practices that systematically exclude culturally different parent groups from being involved in important decisions about the education of their children.	Changes to meet diverse student needs are seen as against the status quo and the assimilation of different cultural groups.	School staff supports and sponsors traditional parent and community organizations and governmental mandates, believing they serve all cultural groups.	Recognizing parent and community needs as they arise, parent, community, and school leaders may develop structures to respond to the needs.	Create structures that address the diverse cultural needs of the school, parents, and community groups and assess effectiveness in meeting those needs.	Parent and community groups provide ongoing meaningful contributions to decisions, policies, and practices that serves the diverse needs of the community.

How to read Table 6.4, the parent and community communication and outreach rubric:

- Note the rubric is composed of rows and columns.
- Each of the rows is one of the five standards referred to as an essential element of cultural competence.
- There are seven columns. At the top of the first column is the title "essential elements." A brief description of the element is given in the context of the working with parents and community topic.
- Each of the next six columns is one of the six points of the cultural proficiency continuum.
- The fifth column is titled cultural competence. Each of the descriptors in that column describes one of the essential elements of cultural competence. The language is in active voice and describes actions that can be taken today in schools.
- The sixth column is titled "cultural proficiency." The description is future focused and measurable.

■ Reflection

What do you see as the main difference between the practices described on the right side of the rubric and the practices described on the left side of the rubric?

In using this cultural proficiency rubric as a key to unlocking our unawareness and opening our minds to possibilities for educating students with whom we have not been successful, what possibilities do you see for educating all student demographic groups to high levels that you did not see before?

How might you be able to use this tool in your professional practice?

_____

_____

_____

_____

■ Professional Development Rubric

Table 6.5 presents the professional development rubric. When you read the descriptions under the "professional development"

Table 6.5 Professional Development Rubric

	Cultural Destructiveness	Cultural Incapacity	Cultural Blindness	Cultural Precompetence	Cultural Competence	Cultural Proficiency
Assessing Cultural Knowledge Extent to which professional development addresses issues of cultural identity.	Professional learning that provides opportunities to learn about one's own and others' cultural identities is avoided and prohibited.	Professional learning promotes practices and approaches that promote assimilation to the dominant culture.	Professional learning provides common approaches that avoid issues related to cultural identity believed to be beneficial to all students.	Recognizing differences between the culture of the home and the culture of the school, professional development may address issues of culture.	Professional learning informs participants about their culture, the cultures of others, and the school's culture. Professional development helps close gaps in achievement and bridge gaps in cultural, linguistic, learning, and communication styles.	Professional learning helps staff close achievement gaps for underserved groups and anticipate changing community needs.
Valuing Diversity Extent to which professional development addresses cultural issues.	Professional learning opportunities intend to extinguish manifestations of culture, language, or learning styles.	Professional learning opportunities support assimilation to the dominant culture and learning styles.	Professional learning opportunities promote one approach to meet the needs of all students.	Recognizes community diversity and may address the needs of different cultural groups in professional learning.	Professional learning helps staff develop approaches that meet the needs of multiple cultural, linguistic, and learning styles.	Professional learning opportunities help participants anticipate, identify, and respond to changing demographics.

92

	Cultural Destructiveness	Cultural Incapacity	Cultural Blindness	Cultural Precompetence	Cultural Competence	Cultural Proficiency
Managing the Dynamics of Difference Extent to which professional development promotes and models the use of inquiry and dialogue related to multiple perspectives and issues arising from diversity.	Professional learning provokes and foments opportunities to denigrate the cultural needs of some student, parent, or staff groups.	Professional learning is used to influence and shape practices that expect others to assimilate to the dominant culture in order to better educate and conserve the resources of the school or district. Processes are justified by *majority rule or opinion.*	Professional learning and meetings advocate topics and processes that promote the common good, and consensus is favored when conflict arises.	Recognizing that issues arising from diversity are ever-present and often provoke conflict, school leaders may identify and develop professional development opportunities that surface multiple perspectives about issues arising from diversity.	Professional learning opportunities incorporate multiple perspectives on relevant topics and build capacity for dialogue about conflict from issues that may arise from issues related to diversity.	Professional learning opportunities promote social action to better meet the needs of an ever-changing community.
Adapting to Diversity Extent to which professional learning facilitates change	Professional learning activities suppress change to meet the needs of a diverse community.	Professional learning opportunities assume that the best way to meet the	Believing they serve the needs of all cultural groups, professional learning	Recognizing the needs of a diverse community, professional learning opportunities	Professional learning opportunities use data to drive change to better meet the needs	Professional learning opportunities help staff anticipate the needs of a changing community and

(Continued)

Table 6.5 (Continued)

	Cultural Destructiveness	Cultural Incapacity	Cultural Blindness	Cultural Precompetence	Cultural Competence	Cultural Proficiency
to meet the needs of the community.		needs of a diverse community is to maintain the status quo and help others to assimilate.	opportunities consist mainly of programs sanctioned by local, state, and federal agencies.	examine and alter practices that may better meet the needs of a diverse community.	of a diverse community.	develop flexible policies and practices to meet current and future needs.
Institutionalizing Cultural Knowledge Extent to which professional development shapes policies and practices that meet the needs of a diverse community.	Professional learning opportunities shaped by values and policies that deny the needs of a diverse school community are systematically applied in schools and classrooms.	Professional learning opportunities that reinforce values and policies ensuring assimilation are applied in classrooms and schools.	Believing they serve the needs of all cultural groups, mandated professional learning opportunities are applied in classrooms and schools.	Recognizing that some community needs are not met, professional learning opportunities may examine and shape values and policies to meet identified needs.	Professional learning opportunities are encouraged, shared, and applied in classrooms, the school, and community for the purpose of improving student learning and achievement.	Professional learning opportunities lead to improving community welfare and interdependence.

column from Table 6.1, as with the previous rubrics you will notice that the descriptions are imported into the first column of Table 6.5. The section that follows the table is designed to guide you in how to read the rubric.

How to read Table 6.5, the professional development rubric:

- Note the rubric is composed of rows and columns.
- Each of the rows is one of the five standards referred to as an essential element of cultural competence.
- There are seven columns. At the top of the first column is the title "essential elements." A brief description of the element is given in the context of the professional development topic.
- Each of the next six columns is one of the six points of the cultural proficiency continuum.
- The fifth column is titled "cultural competence." Each of the descriptors in that column describes one of the essential elements of cultural competence. The language is in active voice and describes actions that can be taken today in schools.
- The sixth column is titled "cultural proficiency." The description is future focused and measurable.

■ Reflection

What do you see as the main difference between the practices described on the right side of the rubric and the practices described on the left side of the rubric?

In using this cultural proficiency rubric as a key to unlocking our unawareness and opening our minds to possibilities for educating students with whom we have not been successful, what possibilities do you see for educating all student demographic groups to high levels that you did not see before?

How might you be able to use this tool in your professional practice?

_____

_____

_____

_____

Because they describe practices at all levels of the continuum, the rubrics for culturally proficient inquiry are tools for both assessing your progress and describing your next steps. They can provide you important information about the strengths and needs of one subsystem or leverage point or about your progress with educational equity across the system. The most important function of the rubrics is for them to inform conversations about our professional practices in seeking ways to ever better serve all students.

Alvin Toffler (2006) admonishes that the illiterate of the twenty-first century will not be those who cannot read and write, but those who cannot learn, unlearn, and relearn. The cultural proficiency rubrics are the keys to our unlearning and our relearning. They give us the opportunity to confront and overcome the inequities that persist in our schools and society. How might we use them to open the doors to possibilities for all of our students?

Note on the Expert Validation of the Cultural Proficiency Rubrics

We submitted the four rubrics to a panel of six educational experts across the United States for their review. Each panelist is familiar with the four tools of cultural proficiency, has published material using the tools of cultural proficiency, and uses cultural proficiency in his or her professional work.

Panelists were provided a matrix of operational definitions (e.g., cultural destructiveness, valuing diversity, professional development) and a matrix that demonstrated the intersections of the continuum and the essential elements tools. The readers were informed that these two documents informed the manner in which the four rubrics were developed.

Panelists were instructed to judge the extent to which each of the cells in the rows (i.e., points of the continuum) were independent and progressive by assigning a numerical score. A rubric was provided to guide judgments. Then, panelists were instructed to judge the essential elements in each cell in the rows as being appropriate descriptions of that point on the continuum for the subject of the rubric (e.g., assessment and accountability). The authors used the judgments from the expert panel to further modify the examples for each of the rubrics.

Part III

The ABC Case Study School and Your School

Culturally Proficient Inquiry Uses Skills You Already Possess

Part III presents a systematic approach for you to study your own school to identify what is currently working well and those areas where improvement is needed. Please note that we use a consistent frame of reference throughout the book, *your school.* You have the choice of applying the tools in this book to your classroom, your grade level, your department, your school, your regional cluster of schools, or your school district.

The fact that you are reading this book indicates that you have joined the many responsible educators (e.g., DuFour, 2004; Haycock, 2001; Johnson, 2002; Reeves, 2000; Singleton, 2006) who are confronting the achievement gaps that abide in our schools. We believe that to make the necessary improvements in our schools, we must know where we are at this point in time in order to develop coherent, cohesive plans for improvement.

Figure III.1 on the following page builds on the information in the introduction to the previous parts (Figures I.1 and II.1), serves to introduce Chapters 7 to 10, and guides you in collecting data about your school to direct your decision making.

Chapters 7, 8, and 9 build on the data described in Part II in two ways. Chapter 7 focuses on student achievement data, and Chapters 8 and 9 focus on student access data. In Chapters 7, 8, and 9, we present the ABC Case Study School's tabulated data. Then, we present blank tables and an accompanying CD for your use. These chapters provide you the tools to:

- Identify the demographic groups you wish to study in your school.
- Pose key questions about the demographic groups under study.
- Analyze and reflect on the data in order to begin the process of understanding the current state of education for the demographic groups of students in your school.

Chapter 10 provides you with another set of tools with which to examine and understand your school. Whereas Chapters 7, 8, and 9 focus on student patterns, Chapter 10 focuses on our practices as educators. You are reintroduced to two of the tools of Cultural Proficiency, the *Cultural Proficiency Continuum* and the *Five Essential Elements of Cultural Competence.* In the same manner that Chapters 7, 8, and 9 provide you with tools to understand and make sense of student achievement data, Chapter 10 provides you with tools to develop and make meaning of conversations you have in your school. When you finish this chapter you will have tools to enhance your understanding of four functions in your school described as leverage points for change:

- Assessment and Accountability,
- Curriculum and Instruction,
- Parent and Community Communications and Outreach, and
- Professional Development.

Chapter 10 continues with the ABC Case Study School and provides a guided tour in applying the rubrics to your school. The chapter describes conversations that might occur in your school about your students. We educators must be able to *hear* how we talk about our students and their cultures and to recognize how our conversation reflects our expectations of and relationships with students and their communities. When combined with the data from Chapters 7, 8, and 9, a powerful profile identifies three aspects of schooling over which we exercise control—curriculum, instruction (i.e., pedagogy), and cultural understanding.

Figure III.1 continues building on the information begun with Figures I.1 and II.1 by providing a pictorial representation of Culturally Proficient Inquiry organized around three data sets—student achievement, student access, and profiles of adult conversations about students identified as underperforming.

The Appendix provides a more technical model for analyzing achievement gap information intended for experienced researchers and evaluators.

Figure III.1   Culturally Proficient Inquiry

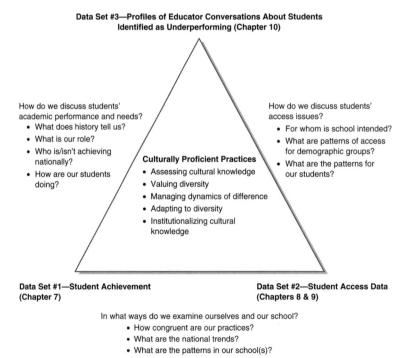

7

Data Set #1

Finding Meaning in
Achievement Data

Let us not be content to wait and see what will
happen, but give us the determination to make the
right things happen.

—Horace Mann (2006)

Getting Centered

In the opening to Chapter 4, you were invited to jot down how you know some students are not performing well and how you know this to be true. Please continue with that line of thinking. Now that you have read more in this book and have had time to think about your students, what more do you know about students who are not achieving well?

_____

_____

_____

_____

Data can support school leaders in crafting authentic visions inclusive of all students. Reeves (2006) believes effective school leaders cut through the "baloney" of vision statements crafted as public relations statements when they can respond to these questions:

- Where are we headed as an organization this year?
- Where will we be three to five years from now?
- What parts of our organization will be the same, and what will change?
- Will there still be a place for me in the future?
- How will my work change?
- What will I need to learn in order to be more valuable to the organization in the future?
- Why will I still want to be a part of this organization in the future? (p. 36)

Responses to questions such as these are needed if educators are to be serious in providing equitable access to all students. Educational leaders who pose such questions to themselves and to all other educators in their schools are engaged in meaningful reflection on their practice, whether it be as a teacher, an aide, a counselor, or an administrator.

This chapter initiates the cultural proficiency inquiry process of gathering data about your school described in Chapters 5 and 6. Data are fundamental to schools being authentic learning organizations. More than anything else, this chapter empowers you to use data to guide your decision making, whether the data are academic achievement test scores, student access issues, or profiles of adult conversation about students in your school. One of the most important questions we can ask is, "Now that we have the data, so what?" The "so what" question is fundamental to making the data useful for improving student learning, and it takes us full circle back to the appropriately provocative questions Reeves (2006) posed above.

Absent proper use, data have limited utility. It is our using data to inform our practices and policies that gives data power. This chapter guides you to compile your school's achievement data. Chapters 8 and 9 provide the opportunity to compile and analyze student access data for your school.

The achievement data analyses in this chapter focus on standards-based and norm-referenced tests. These tests are typically found in state and accountability programs, and as such, results are readily available at district and site levels. Additionally, we strongly encourage you to use other sources of achievement data available at your school, such as ongoing classroom formative assessments and other measures of student achievement related to student learning. Local assessment measures often are a better reflection of student achievement of your school's curriculum and certainly will provide a rich, comprehensive perspective on student achievement. Remember, it is always best to have multiple measures of student achievement when assessing student performance. The method of analysis presented in this book readily applies to these additional assessments.

This chapter uses the recommended peer group model for analyzing student achievement gaps. A unique feature of the peer group model approach to data analysis is that English learners are not included in tables focusing on Latino students. Therefore, no students are represented in both groups for an analysis of achievement patterns.

The Peer Group Model and the ABC Case Study School

In Chapter 4 we introduced the peer group model as a way to compare students in one group to all other students (i.e., their peers) at your school. The peer group model approach represents a more valid comparison of student achievement gaps within a school or district or social context. This context is reflective of local student demographics and incorporates more of the student population in the achievement gap analysis, as you will see in our case study school.

We use a case study school to illustrate how to compute group scores and interpret demographic group differences.[1] The ABC Case Study School is located in a suburban area in California. It serves students in kindergarten through sixth grade. The ABC Case Study School is a Title I school with 571 students. It is in its second year as a designated state and federal program improvement site. Tables 7.1 and 7.2 note the student demographics for the ABC Case Study School. Table 7.1 lists student enrollment by student race-ethnicity.

Table 7.2 lists student enrollment by gender, poverty level, English learner (EL), and primary languages of the majority of EL students. Students identified for inclusion as poverty level are students who participate in the National School Lunch Program (NSLP). Demographics for this chapter are based primarily on the October 2004 California Basic Educational Data System (CBEDS) count.

---

1. A more sophisticated approach to identifying significant educational differences is provided in the Appendix.

Table 7.1   Student Enrollment by Race-Ethnicity of ABC Students

Ethnicity	Number of Students	Percent Enrollment
African American	60	10.5%
First Nations	10	1.8%
Asian	24	4.2%
Filipino	7	1.2%
Hispanic/Latino	159	27.8%
Pacific Islander	7	1.2%
White (Not Hispanic)	304	53.2%

Table 7.2   Additional Descriptive Information of ABC Students

Group Characteristics	Number of Students	Percent Enrollment
Gender		
Males	292	52.9%
Females	260	47.1%
SES and EL		
NSLP	407	73.8%
English Learners	145	25.4%
Primary Language of EL		
Spanish	113	77.9%
Russian	9	6.2%
Farsi	4	2.8%
Ukrainian	4	2.8%
Students With Disabilities	58	10.2%

The ABC Case Study School, like many schools in the United States, has a diverse student population with three or more predominant racial-ethnic groups, in this case Hispanic/Latino, African American, and white. Similar to many schools throughout the United States, approximately 25% of the students are English learners and about 10% of the students have been identified with learning disabilities. Spanish is the predominant primary language of English learners in the ABC School, an increasingly similar pattern across the country.

Content Standards-Based Assessments

Too often the conversations among educators, when applying state and local standards, imply deficiency on the part of the student. We find that culturally proficient educators focus on what **we** need to learn to better serve our students. As you continue in this and subsequent chapters, our consistent question is, "How does this information inform our practices as educators?" Your role as an administrator, a teacher, a counselor, an aide, a parent, or a member of the community is enhanced when framed with what we need to know or learn in order to be effective in educating all children and youth. Content-based assessments are our first opportunity to extend our learning.

The most readily available student score for content standards-based tests are performance levels. Performance levels vary from state to state or district to district, but typically consist of four to five mastery levels. For example, a five-level performance scale is frequently represented by performance-level descriptors such as "advanced," "proficient," "basic," "below basic," and "far below basic." In the following analysis, we have combined these five performance levels into three performance ranges to facilitate making curricular and instruction decisions:

- percent scoring at advanced or proficient level,
- percent scoring at basic level,
- percent scoring at below or far below basic level.

For schools using a four-point performance scale, the four levels can usually be combined into three levels as we have done in this illustration. Four-level rubrics usually include two levels representing "proficient" and "advanced" and are usually defined as students meeting state or local standards. Students scoring "basic" are usually defined as marginally meeting state or local standards. Students scoring "below basic" or "far below basic" are usually defined as the students scoring below state or local standards and in need of some type of instructional intervention.

To determine the differences between two student groups, we begin by determining the two demographic groups of students to be compared (e.g., male and female students). Next, we identify the percentage of male and female students who score at each of the three performance levels. The percentages of students scoring at these three levels are used to compare, in our example male and female students, to determine whether there is an achievement gap.

We need to establish a criterion to determine whether there are educationally significant differences between the groups. As you may recall from Chapter 3, we recommended using an effect size of 0.25 (i.e., 10 percentile points) or more to determine an educationally significant difference between two groups. We define educationally significant difference as a difference that has practical educational implications representing an existing achievement gap between the groups and the need for additional instructional strategies or interventions and cultural responsiveness to the needs of your students. This is a judgment decision, and you can apply a criterion level other than 10% if you feel that is more appropriate for your setting. A 10% criterion may be a conservative criterion and your school may wish to use a lower figure (e.g., 5%) to identify differences between groups.

ABC School's Content Standards-Based Assessment

The ABC Case Study School provides an illustration of the data collection process and analysis of a standards-based test. After the case study review, we provide space for you to record your school's data and reflect your observations about student demographic group performance at your school. The ABC Case Study educators chose the peer group model for the analysis. The educators completed an analysis for the following student groups: African American, Latino, White, poverty, gender, and English language learners. For illustrative purposes, the comparisons between the following groups are included in this chapter:

- African American students with their African American peer group students (i.e., non-African American students),
- Latino students compared with the Latino student peer group, and
- Female and male students.

To provide a more reliable analysis, data for English learners were considered in a separate analysis. You will recall from the discussion in Chapter 3 that because not all Latino students are English learners, they are considered in separate comparisons to provide for a more accurate assessment of each group's educational needs. Results are also displayed by grade level to enable a diagnostic look at student performance across grade levels. Results are presented only for English language arts. The same process should be applied to other content areas, such as mathematics and science, and to other demographic student comparison groups.

■ African American Student Group Compared to African American Peer Group

Tables 7.3 and 7.4 display African American student and African American peer group achievement on a standards-based English language arts test by grade level and for the total group (all grade levels combined). In keeping with the peer group model approach to data analysis, English learners are not included in this table and the two demographic groups are dichotomous in that no one student is represented in both groups in this analysis.

Table 7.3   Standards-Based English Language Arts: Number and Percent Students in African American Subgroup, ABC Case Study School

	African American Students					
	Grade 2	*Grade 3*	*Grade 4*	*Grade 5*	*Grade 6*	*Total*
Advanced						
Number	0	1	1	1	0	3
Percent	0%	11%	10%	9%	0%	6%
Proficient						
Number	2	2	3	3	1	11
Percent	25%	22%	30%	27%	11%	23%
Basic						
Number	2	2	1	3	3	11
Percent	25%	22%	10%	27%	33%	23%
Below Basic						
Number	3	3	4	2	4	16
Percent	38%	33%	40%	18%	44%	34%
Far Below Basic						
Number	1	1	1	2	1	6
Percent	13%	11%	10%	18%	11%	13%
Total						
Number	8	9	10	11	9	47
Percent	100%	100%	100%	100%	100%	100%

Tables 7.3 and 7.4 include the number and percent of students scoring at each performance level by grade level. The tables present data for five levels of performance and are summarized into three groups for comparison purposes in Table 7.5.

Table 7.5 summarizes the performance of the African American students and the African American peer group students from Tables 7.3 and 7.4 to provide for ease of analysis. As we previously noted, this

Table 7.4   Standards-Based English Language Arts: Number and Percent Students in African American Peer Subgroup, ABC Case Study School

	African American Peer Group Students					
	Grade 2	Grade 3	Grade 4	Grade 5	Grade 6	Total
Advanced						
Number	0	7	6	3	5	21
Percent	0%	16%	13%	8%	9%	9%
Proficient						
Number	14	12	20	16	18	80
Percent	38%	27%	43%	40%	33%	36%
Basic						
Number	9	20	13	10	25	77
Percent	24%	44%	28%	25%	45%	34%
Below Basic						
Number	11	3	4	5	5	28
Percent	30%	7%	9%	13%	9%	13%
Far Below Basic						
Number	3	3	4	6	2	18
Percent	8%	7%	9%	15%	4%	8%
Total						
Number	37	45	47	40	55	224
Percent	100%	100%	100%	100%	100%	100%

Table 7.5   Summary of English Language Arts Standards Test for Total Group African American and African American Peer Group Students by Combining Performance Levels, ABC Case Study School

Subgroup	Percent Advanced or Proficient	Percent Basic	Percent Below or Far Below Basic
African American	29%	23%	47%
African American Peer Group	45%	34%	21%

summary combines student performance from five to three performance levels for the total group.

Table 7.5 indicates that the African American peer group has a larger percentage of students scoring in the advanced or proficient range (45% compared to 29%) and scoring at the basic range (34% compared to 23%). African American students have a greater percentage of students scoring at the below or far below basic range (47% compared to 21%).

These percentages represent an educationally significant difference between the African American and African American peer group students at all three performance bands. All three exceed a 10% difference, with the largest difference being at the below and far below basic range, with 26% (47% minus 21%) more African American students scoring in this band. The differences at the first and second bands indicated the following findings: a 16% difference between African American students and their peers at the advanced or proficient levels and a 11% difference between the two subgroups at the basic level.

Conclusion

An educationally significant achievement gap exists between African American students and the African American peer group at this school. The magnitude of this difference was most apparent for students scoring in the below and far below basic range.

Grade-Level Comparisons

Data from the ABC Case Study School provides the opportunity to call attention to an important caution when comparing demographic group data. One must be careful in interpreting *grade-level* patterns from the ABC School data because of the small number of students at each grade level for African American students (numbers of students range from 8 to 11). The ABC Case Study School does not provide a large enough sample size (30 or more students) to determine grade-level trends for the African American students.

■ Latino Students Compared to Latino Peer Group Students

Tables 7.6 and 7.7 represent Latino student and Latino peer group student achievement on the same standards-based English language arts test for grades 2 through 6. Again, keeping with the peer group model approach to data analysis, English learners' performance was analyzed separately and their data are not included in these tables.

Table 7.6   Standards-Based English Language Arts: Number and Percent Students of Latino Students, ABC Case Study School

	Latino Students					
	Grade 2	Grade 3	Grade 4	Grade 5	Grade 6	Total
Advanced						
Number	0	2	0	0	1	3
Percent	0%	20%	0%	0%	7%	6%
Proficient						
Number	3	1	7	4	4	19
Percent	30%	10%	58%	50%	29%	35%
Basic						
Number	2	6	1	2	8	19
Percent	20%	60%	8%	25%	57%	35%
Below Basic						
Number	4	1	2	0	1	8
Percent	40%	10%	17%	0%	7%	15%
Far Below Basic						
Number	1	0	2	2	0	5
Percent	10%	0%	17%	25%	0%	9%
Total						
Number	10	10	12	8	14	54
Percent	100%	100%	100%	100%	100%	100%

The Latino and Latino peer group students in Tables 7.6 and 7.7 are dichotomous, with no students being represented in both groups. These tables include the number and percentage of students scoring at each performance level by grade level.

Table 7.8 summarizes the performance of the Latino and Latino peer group students for all students (total). This table combines student performance from five to three performance levels.

Table 7.8 indicates that the differences between the Latino student group and the Latino peer group range from 2% (proficient/advanced and below/far below basic) to 3% (basic). These represent minimal differences between the subgroups and, therefore, do not represent educationally significant differences in student achievement.

Table 7.7 Standards-Based English Language Arts: Number and Percent Students of Latino Peer Group Students

	Latino Peer Group Students					
	Grade 2	Grade 3	Grade 4	Grade 5	Grade 6	Total
Advanced						
Number	0	6	7	4	4	21
Percent	0%	14%	16%	9%	8%	10%
Proficient						
Number	13	13	16	15	15	72
Percent	37%	30%	36%	35%	30%	33%
Basic						
Number	9	16	13	11	20	69
Percent	26%	36%	29%	26%	40%	32%
Below Basic						
Number	10	5	6	7	8	36
Percent	29%	11%	13%	16%	16%	17%
Far Below Basic						
Number	3	4	3	6	3	19
Percent	9%	9%	7%	14%	6%	9%
Total						
Number	35	44	45	43	50	217
Percent	100%	100%	100%	100%	100%	100%

Table 7.8 Summary of English Language Arts Standards Test for Total Group Latino and Latino Peer Group Students by Combining Performance Levels, ABC Case Study School

Subgroup	Percent Advanced or Proficient	Percent Basic	Percent Below or Far Below Basic
Latino	41%	35%	24%
Latino Peer Group	43%	32%	26%

Conclusion

No educationally significant achievement gap exists between Latino students and the Latino peer group on this English language arts standards-based test.

Grade-Level Comparisons

Again, ABC Case Study School does not provide a large enough sample size (i.e., ranging from 8 to 14 students) to determine grade-level trends for the Latino students.

Importance of Removing Data About
English Learners From the Peer Group Analysis

Table 7.9 includes a summary of the Latino group compared to the Latino peer group *including* English learners. The data are an illustration of the importance of removing data about English learners from this achievement gap analysis in order to get a true picture of student needs. In contrasting the findings between Tables 7.7 and 7.8, it is easy to see that the school is educating Latino and Latino peer group students comparably but is struggling with its English learner students.

Based on this information, there is an educationally significant difference, and therefore an achievement gap, between Latino students and their peer group. This conclusion does not accurately describe the achievement of Latino students at ABC Case Study School because it does not address the specific learning needs of Latino English-speaking and Latino non-English-speaking students. The differences in performance between the groups in Table 7.9 are 17% at the advanced/proficient level and 16% at the below/far below basic levels.

Table 7.9   Summary of English Language Arts Standards Test by Combined Performance Levels Including English Learners, ABC Case Study School

Demographic Group	*Percent Advanced or Proficient*	*Percent Basic*	*Percent Below or Far Below Basic*
Latino With English Language Learners Included	23%	35%	42%
Latino Peers With English Language Learners Included	40%	34%	26%

■ Male Students Compared to Female Students

Tables 7.10 and 7.11 display male and female peer group achievement on a standards-based English language arts test at each performance level by grade and for the total group. In keeping with the peer group model approach to data analysis, English learners are not included in this table and the two demographic groups are dichotomous in that no students are represented in both groups in this analysis.

Tables 7.10 and 7.11 include the number and percentage of male and female students scoring at each performance level by grade level. Notice that these tables present data for five levels of performance and are summarized into three groups for comparison purposes in Table 7.12.

Table 7.12 combines the performance of male and female students from Tables 7.10 and 7.11 for ease of analysis. As previously noted, this summary combines student performance from five to three performance levels for all grade levels combined.

Conclusion

No educationally significant achievement gap was noted between male and female students on this English language arts standards-based test. The differences between the two groups varied from 1% to 5% for the three combined performance levels.

Table 7.10   Standards-Based English Language Arts: Number and Percent Students in Male and Female Students, ABC Case Study School

	Male Students					
	Grade 2	*Grade 3*	*Grade 4*	*Grade 5*	*Grade 6*	*Total*
Advanced						
Number	0	6	0	2	3	3
Percent	0%	20%	0%	7%	10%	7%
Proficient						
Number	14	8	14	14	6	11
Percent	44%	27%	47%	47%	20%	37%
Basic						
Number	5	11	9	7	13	45
Percent	16%	37%	30%	23%	43%	30%
Below Basic						
Number	13	4	4	0	5	26
Percent	41%	13%	13%	0%	17%	17%
Far Below Basic						
Number	0	1	3	7	3	14
Percent	0%	3%	10%	23%	10%	9%
Total						
Number	32	30	30	30	30	152
Percent	100%	100%	100%	100%	100%	100%

Table 7.11 Standards-Based English Language Arts: Number and Percent Students in Male and Female Students, ABC Case Study School

	Female Students					
	Grade 2	Grade 3	Grade 4	Grade 5	Grade 6	Total
Advanced						
Number	1	3	7	3	2	16
Percent	3%	10%	23%	9%	6%	10%
Proficient						
Number	8	7	10	10	13	48
Percent	26%	23%	33%	31%	38%	30%
Basic						
Number	11	14	6	9	15	55
Percent	35%	45%	20%	28%	44%	35%
Below Basic						
Number	6	4	5	7	4	26
Percent	19%	13%	17%	22%	12%	16%
Far Below Basic						
Number	5	3	2	3	0	13
Percent	16%	10%	7%	9%	0%	8%
Total						
Number	31	31	30	32	34	158
Percent	100%	100%	100%	100%	100%	100%

Table 7.12 Summary of English Language Arts Standards Test for Total Group Male and Female Students by Combining Performance Levels, ABC Case Study School

Demographic Group	Percent Advanced or Proficient	Percent Basic	Percent Below or Far Below Basic
Males	44%	30%	26%
Female	41%	35%	25%

Grade-Level Comparisons

Because there are 30 or more male and female students at each grade level, a grade-level comparison is appropriate. Observations from the grade-level comparisons are as follows:

1. Grade-level patterns by grade level indicate that male students are scoring proficient or advanced by a larger per-cent (10% or more) at grades 2, 3, and 5. The difference in favor of the males is 15%, 14%, and 14%, respectively. Female students outperform male students at Grade 6 by 14%.

2. Grade-level patterns for students scoring in the below and far below basic levels are similar for male and female students. However, only 12% of female students score in this range at Grade 6 compared to 27% for male students. Therefore, the sixth-grade trend overall shows better performance at the high and low performance levels for female students.

Now It Is *Your Turn:* Entering Your School's Standards-Based Assessment Data

The following tables are available for you to enter your school's student achievement data. You will need to determine the grade levels for which you have content standards data and select the pairs of demographic groups that you wish to compare. Do not select a subgroup unless it has a total (all grade levels combined) of at least 30 students for this analysis. These tables are included on the CD that accompanies this book. If you are completing your calculations with-out the use of the CD, then use the blank form on the CD under the Data Collection and Entry Files referred to as Chapter 7—7.13 and 7.14. If you are using the CD to enter and calculate your results, then use the file found under the Data Computation Files and referred to as Chapter 7—standards assessment—ELA and mathematics.

■ Directions

1. Enter the number of students for each demographic group that scored in the five performance levels for each grade. Please note that Table 7.13 is for one identified group and Table 7.14 for their peer group.

2. To compute the totals and percentages for your school, you can use the CD provided. If you fill in your numbers on the CD, it will automatically compute the values for you. You can also compute these totals with a calculator if you prefer.

Table 7.13   Standards-Based Test_____: Number and Percent Students of
                 (Demographic Group)_____ Students, _____School

Demographic Group: _____
Content Area: _____

	Grade	*Grade*	*Grade*	*Grade*	*Grade*	*Total*
Advanced						
Number						
Percent						
Proficient						
Number						
Percent						
Basic						
Number						
Percent						
Below Basic						
Number						
Percent						
Far Below Basic						
Number						
Percent						
Total						
Number						
Percent						

Table 7.14   Standards-Based Test_____: Number and Percent Students of (Demographic Group)_____Students, _____School

Demographic Group: _____
Content Area: _____

	Grade	*Grade*	*Grade*	*Grade*	*Grade*	*Total*
Advanced						
Number						
Percent						
Proficient						
Number						
Percent						
Basic						
Number						
Percent						
Below Basic						
Number						
Percent						
Far Below Basic						
Number						
Percent						
Total						
Number						
Percent						

After entering the data in these tables, total the percentage of students who scored in the three performance bands for both demographic groups in Table 7.15. If you used the enclosed CD, these will be computed for you and you can enter the information into Table 7.15. If you did not use the CD for calculations, then this table is available to record your scores under the Data Collection and Entry Forms—Chapter 7—Table 7.15. This information will be used to determine whether there are educationally significant differences between the two groups and, if so, the magnitude of the differences.

Table 7.15 Summary of _____Standards Test for Total Group _____and _____Peer Group Students by Combining Performance Levels, _____School

Demographic group	Percent Advanced or Proficient	Percent Basic	Percent Below or Far Below Basic
_____ Group			
_____ Peer Group			

■ Student-Focused Dialogue Using Achievement Data

Questions to explore when examining your school's data are as follows:

Are there significant differences between the demographic groups? Is so, at what performance levels?

_____

_____

_____

_____

What is the extent of the differences? Do they vary by performance bands?

_____

_____

_____

_____

Do you see any patterns that might be evident when you explore your grade-level scores? If so, what are these differences? Remember that some grade levels may have a small number of students, so be careful in your interpretation.

_____

_____

_____

_____

What conclusions do you draw from the data?

_____

_____

_____

_____

■ Another Data Source: Norm-Referenced Assessments

Norm-referenced tests are frequently used as part of a state or districts' accountability system. Scores most readily available at the school-site level are percentile scores or normal curve equivalent scores (NCEs).

To determine whether there are educationally significant differences between two student demographic groups at your school, first determine the percentage of students who score in each of the four quartile bands. The four quartile bands are

- first quartile band—scores from the 1st to 25th percentile;
- second quartile band—scores from the 26th to 49th percentile;
- third quartile band—scores from the 50th to 74th percentile; and
- fourth quartile band—scores from the 75th to 99th percentile.

Students scoring in the third and fourth quartile bands are scoring at or above the national norm group, whereas students scoring in the first and second quartile bands are scoring below the national norm. The 50th percentile on a norm-referenced test is considered average. The percentage of students scoring in these four levels is used to compare two demographic groups to see if there is an achievement gap between the groups. We recommend using the 10% difference to determine whether there is an educationally significant difference between the groups. This 10% difference applies for each of the quartile ranges. If NCEs are available, then the four quartile bands are defined as

- first quartile band—NCEs from 1 to 36;
- second quartile band—NCEs from 37 to 49;
- third quartile band—NCEs from 50 to 64; and
- fourth quartile band—NCEs from 65 to 99.

■ Norm-Referenced Data ABC Case Study School

This case study continues with data from the same elementary school where a norm-referenced test is administered at Grade 3. It includes a comparison between poverty and nonpoverty students. Poverty is defined as student participation in the National School Lunch Program. The test used is the California Achievement Test—6th Edition in Reading. Consistent with the peer group model, English learners are removed from this analysis and considered separately to provide more accurate assessment of their needs. The same format can be used with other peer groups and in other tested content areas. Table 7.16 notes the percentage of students scoring at each quartile from both the poverty and nonpoverty peer group. Also noted is the difference in percentage of students scoring at each quartile for the two groups.

As you can see from examining Table 7.16, the differences between students from the poverty and nonpoverty groups range from 12% to 15% for the four quartile bands. These differences are considered to be educationally significant because each exceeds the 10% criterion. A lower percentage of students from poverty backgrounds scored above the national average (i.e., above the 50th percentile in the third and fourth quartiles), and a higher percentage scored below the 50th percentile (i.e., in the first and second quartiles). Fifty percent of students from poverty backgrounds placed above the 50th percentile, well below the 77% of the students from the nonpoverty peer group. The other 50% of students from poverty backgrounds were below the 50th percentile (i.e., in the first and second quartiles), whereas only 23% of students from the nonpoverty peer group were below the 50th percentile.

Table 7.16   Norm-Referenced Test in Third Grade Reading: Number and Percent
                   Students in Poverty and Nonpoverty Peer Subgroups, ABC Case Study School

	Grade 3 Reading		
	Poverty	Nonpoverty	Difference
4th Quartile			
Number	9	12	
Percent	28%	40%	12%
3rd Quartile			
Number	7	11	
Percent	22%	37%	15%
2nd Quartile			
Number	8	4	
Percent	25%	13%	12%
1st Quartile			
Number	8	3	
Percent	25%	10%	15%
Total			
Number	32	30	
Percent	100%	100%	

Conclusion

An educationally significant achievement gap exists between
students from poverty and nonpoverty students on the reading norm-
referenced test. This difference was noted at all quartile ranges.

Your Turn: Entering Your School's Norm-Referenced Assessment Data

Tables 7.17 and 7.18 are available for you to enter your school's student
achievement data. Determine the grade levels for which you have
norm-referenced test data and select the pairs of demographic groups
that you wish to compare. Caution: Be sure not to select a demographic
group unless it has a total of at least 30 students for this analysis. These
tables are also included on the CD that accompanies this book. If you
are completing your calculations without the use of the CD, then use
the blank form on the CD under the Data Collection and Entry Files

referred to as Chapter 7—7.17 and 7.18. If you are using the CD to enter and calculate your results, then use the file found under the Data Computation Files—Chapter 7 NRT—Reading and Mathematics.

■ Directions

Enter the number of students for each demographic group that scored in the four quartile levels for each grade. To compute the totals for your school and the percentages, you can use to the provided CD. If you fill in your numbers on this CD, it will automatically compute these values for you.

After entering the data in Tables 7.17 and 7.18, total the percentage of students who scored in the quartile bands for both demographic groups of students in Table 7.19. If you use the CD, these will be computed for you. If you did not use the CD for calculations, then this table is available under the Data Collection and Entry Forms—Chapter 7—Table 7.19. Use this information to determine whether there are educationally significant differences between the two subgroups and, if so, the magnitude, or extent, of the differences.

■ Student-Focused Dialogue Using Achievement Data

What is the criterion level you will use in determining differences between groups at your school? Some questions to explore when examining your school's data are as follows:

Are there educationally significant differences between the groups? If so, at what levels?

_____

_____

_____

_____

What is the extent of the differences? Do they vary by performance bands?

_____

_____

_____

_____

Table 7.17   Norm-Referenced Test (Content Area)_____: Number and
Percent Students of (Demographic Group)_____ Students,
_____ School

Demographic Group: _____

Content Area: _____

	Grade	*Grade*	*Grade*	*Grade*	*Grade*	*Total*
75th to 99th Percentile						
Number						
Percent						
50th to 74th Percentile						
Number						
Percent						
26th to 49th Percentile						
Number						
Percent						
1st to 25th Percentile						
Number						
Percent						
Total						
Number						
Percent						

Table 7.18   Norm-Referenced Test (Content Area)_____: Number and
Percent Students (Peer Group)_____ Students _____ School,

Peer Demographic group: _____

	Grade	Grade	Grade	Grade	Grade	Total
75th to 99th Percentile						
Number						
Percent						
50th to 74th Percentile						
Number						
Percent						
26th to 49th Percentile						
Number						
Percent						
1st to 25th Percentile						
Number						
Percent						
Total						
Number						
Percent						

Table 7.19 Summary of _____Norm-Referenced Test for Total Group _____and _____Peer Group Students by Combining Performance Levels, _____School

Subgroup	1st Quartile	2nd Quartile	3rd Quartile	4th Quartile
_____ Group				
_____ Peer Group				

Do you see any trends that might be evident when you explore your grade-level scores? If so, what are these differences?

_____

_____

_____

_____

What conclusions do you draw from these data?

_____

_____

_____

_____

Using the tables you have completed in this chapter, you are ready to summarize your data and begin an analysis of data set #1. Please use Table 7.20 to summarize your findings for achievement data. Table 7.20 is available on the CD under Data Collections and Entry Forms, Chapter 7—Table 7.20. Use the group comparisons that illustrate achievement gaps for your school in this table. You will import the data from Table 7.20 into a table at the end of Chapters 8 and 9 to add student access data to provide an even more informed picture of your students' experience at your school. After summarizing your findings in Table 7.20 and coming to some conclusions based on the data, reflect on the questions in the section that follows.

■ Student-Focused Dialogue Using the Rubrics and Outcomes From Table 7.20

The questions in this section are derived from the rubrics presented in Chapter 6 and are offered here to help you correlate student outcomes with educational practices you believe to be influencing the student outcomes reflected in your data summary. You may find it informative to refer to each rubric in Chapter 6 as you consider the questions.

At the end of Chapter 9 you will have an opportunity to use your reflective questions for Chapters 7, 8, and 9 to shape your analysis of one or more important subsystems or leverage points in order to prioritize your next steps to better meet the needs of underperforming students.

Curriculum and Instruction

Using the curriculum and instruction rubric as a framework, examine the summative data for Table 7.20 and consider the following reflective questions. We provide space at the end of this section for you to record your responses.

- What kinds of experiences are students having in classrooms? Are they engaged in quality opportunities to learn?
- Are they encouraged to contribute their knowledge and perspectives to the learning process, and are their contributions valued? Is learning scaffolded to close gaps between what the student knows and what he or she needs to know? Do the instructional approaches facilitate individual student learning or impede it?
- To what extent are educators other than the classroom teacher aware of and involved in supporting students' progress?

_____

_____

_____

_____

Assessment and Accountability

Using the assessment and accountability rubric as a framework, examine the summative data for Table 7.20 and consider the following reflective questions. We provide space at the end of this section for you to record your responses.

- How are students and educators provided feedback about student progress?
- What opportunities do students have to practice their learning and revise their work?
- What kinds of data do teachers use to inform instructional decisions? How do educators collect and use data about students' progress and important gaps between student groups?
- To what extent do educators share information about student progress and strategies to support the learning needs of underperforming student groups?

_____

_____

_____

_____

Parent and Community Communication and Outreach

Using the parent and community communication and outreach rubric as a framework, examine the summative data for Table 7.20 and consider the following reflective questions. We provide space at the end of this section for you to record your responses.

- To what extent do educators seek and use information about students' home cultures to bridge gaps between the way things are done at home and the expectations of the school?
- How do educators encourage communication and participation from parents in their children's learning?

_____

_____

_____

_____

Professional Development

Using the professional development rubric as a framework, examine the summative data for Table 7.20 and consider the following reflective questions. We provide space at the end of this section for you to record your responses.

- What opportunities do educators have to discuss the connections between culture and learning and to learn how to differentiate instruction and integrate culturally relevant approaches into their curriculum?
- What opportunities and resources does the school provide for teachers to seek and share information and strategies to improve the learning of specific underperforming student groups?

_____

_____

_____

_____

Table 7.20 School Data Summary

| Groups Compared | Standards-Based Test | | Norm-Referenced Test | | | Other Assessments | Other Assessments |
	ELA	Math	Other	ELA	Math		
African American & Peer Group							
Latino & Peer Group							
White & Peer Group							
Poverty & Nonpoverty							
Male & Female							
Others							

8

Data Set #2

Finding Meaning in Student Access Data

It seems like it is less about doing more of what we know and more about finding out what we don't know (and don't know that we don't know).

—Participant in cultural
proficiency session, August 2006

Getting Centered

You have gathered achievement data that describe demographic patterns among your students. Think of your students and what noncurricular issues affect their ability to be successful in school. What impact do you believe the noncurricular issues have on your students? How do you think your students would describe those same issues from their vantage points?

_____

_____

_____

_____

Ray Terrell, our colleague and coauthor of other works on cultural proficiency, has been consistent in advising that change in schools is a "both-and," not an "either-or" construct. He continually advises that the false dichotomies fostered by either-or thinking serve neither the educator nor the students. Because the school is a system comprising numerous subsystems, it is important to understand students' experiences in ways not measured by testing. A complement to student testing is student access data. Consideration of data from testing alongside data about student access provides a powerful both-and examination of our schools.

In this chapter we guide you through a consideration of how students access schools in terms of attendance, suspensions, and special needs program identification. Again, we encourage you to identify other access information that is available to you in completing this analysis. In Chapter 9 we provide an opportunity to display student access data unique to secondary schools.

The determination of educationally significant differences between demographic groups is more challenging when describing access data. We, the authors, have established criteria for each of these access measures to determine whether there are differences between the groups. You should be aware that these criteria are not fixed and should be adjusted for local needs. The challenge in establishing these criteria is to avoid setting them so high that you miss important differences between groups, but not so low that you falsely identify differences between the groups.

In most cases, there is more than one way to compute student access data. On the basis of our experience, we selected approaches that include information that is more readily accessible and usable for school-site staff.

We use the peer group model in analyzing student access data in much the same manner as we did with student achievement data in Chapter 7. This model compares each demographic group to its peer group at its school, analyzes English learners as a distinct demographic group, and includes demographic groups comprising 30 or more students.

Access Data: Student Attendance

One way students' attendance can be measured is by comparing the number of student absences to the number of school days the student was enrolled. This ratio is determined by dividing the number of days each student was absent by the total number of days that the student was enrolled. For example, if a school year is 180 days, then a student who is absent for 15 days would have an absence ratio of 0.083 (i.e., 15/180). This student was absent for 8.3% of the school year.

As with the other measures in Chapter 7, a criterion must be established to determine whether there is an educationally significant difference between the attendance rates of different demographic groups. We suggest that a difference between the rates of two groups of greater than 3% be considered educationally significant. In a 180 school day calendar, 3% represents approximately 5.4 days of instruction. You may choose a different criterion for your students if you find it more appropriate to do so. For example, a 5.6% criterion represents just over 10 days of absence or two weeks of lost instruction.

As in previous examples, the peer group model does not include English learners when analyzing students' ethnic, poverty, and gender comparisons with their peer groups. To better serve the academic needs of English learners, compare their data with their peer group who are all non-English learners.

■ ABC School Case Study for Attendance Data

The average percentages of days demographic groups were absent for the 2004–2005 school year are noted in Table 8.1 for the ABC Case Study School. Table 8.1 includes each demographic group, along with its comparison peer group. Note that Table 8.1 has seven columns of information. Operational definitions for the column headings are

1. *Demographic Groups Being Compared*—the pairs of demographic groups you have selected for your analysis.

2. *Number of Students*—the number of students that are in each demographic group comparison. We suggest that a demographic group has to include 30 or more students to yield reliable data.

3. *Number of Days Enrolled*—the total number of days all students were enrolled at your school during the school year for both demographic groups.

4. *Total Days of Absence*—the sum of days all students in each demographic group were absent during the school year.

5. *Percent of Days Absent*—the total days students were absent (column 4) divided by the total days of enrollment (column 3).

6. *Difference in Percent*—the difference between the two groups being compared from column 5. Therefore, subtract the smaller percent from the larger percent to determine the difference. For example, in Table 8.1 the absence rate for African American students is 8.8%, whereas the absence rate for the peer demographic group is 5.6%, which results in a significant difference of 3.2%.

7. *Educationally Significant Difference?*—determines whether there is a significant difference between demographic groups. If the difference in percent reported in column 6 is greater than 3%, then there is an educationally significant difference and this would be noted by indicating *Yes.* If the difference is 3% or less, then there is no educationally significant difference between the demographic groups and the corresponding notation is *No.* If you chose a criterion different from 3%, note the change you made and then determine whether a significant difference exists.

Conclusion

On the basis of the established criteria, an educationally significant difference exists in demographic group attendance patterns between African American students and their peer group. The African American students had significantly more absences. No educationally significant differences were noted between the other demographic groups.

Your Turn: Entering Your School's Student Subgroup Attendance Data

Table 8.2 is displayed for you to enter your student demographic group attendance data. If you use the CD for data entry, you will only be required to provide information in columns 2, 3, and 4. The CD computation file is located under the Data Computation Files as Chapter 8—Table 8.2. The software will compute the remaining table information for you. If you need to compute the remaining three columns, please refer to the definitions that precede Table 8.1. If you are completing your calculations without the use of the CD, then use the blank form on the CD under the Data Collection and Entry files referred to as Chapter 8—8.2.

Table 8.1 Analysis of Demographic Group Attendance Data, ABC Case Study School

Group (1)	Number of Students (2)	Total Days Enrolled (3)	Total Days Absent (4)	Percent of Days Absent (5)	Difference in Percent (6)	Educationally Significant Difference (More Than 3%)? (7)
African American	109	13431	1186	8.8%	3.2%	Yes
Peer Group	445	61764	3449	5.6%		
Latino	104	14806	733	5.0%	1.5%	No
Peer Group	450	60389	3902	6.5%		
White	299	40566	2345	5.8%	0.8%	No
Peer Group	255	34629	2290	6.6%		
Males	277	37216	2481	6.7%	1.0%	No
Females	277	37979	2154	5.7%		
Poverty	257	34364	2559	7.4%	2.3%	No
Peer Group	292	40750	2068	5.1%		
English Learners	161	24489	977	4.1%	2.1%	No
Peer Group	554	75195	4635	6.2%		

Table 8.2   Analysis of Demographic Group Attendance Data, _____ School

Group (1)	Number of Students (2)	Total Days Enrolled (3)	Total Days Absent (4)	Percent of Days Absent (5)	Difference in Percent (6)	Educationally Significant Difference (More Than 3%)? (7)
African American Peer Group						
Latino Peer Group						
White Peer Group						
Males Females						
Poverty Peer Group						
English Learners Peer Group						
Other Group						

■ Student-Focused Dialogue Using Attendance Data

Some questions to explore when examining your school's attendance data are as follows:

Are there any educationally significant differences between any of your demographic groups? If so, what groups are identified as having an attendance gap?

_____

_____

_____

_____

What is the extent of the differences? Do they vary by demographic groups?

_____

_____

_____

_____

What conclusions do you draw from the data?

_____

_____

_____

_____

Access Data: Student Suspensions

There are several ways student suspension rates can be computed. We have elected to define suspension rates as the total number of days students are suspended during the school year. The total number of days students are suspended is important, as is student attendance, because it represents lost opportunity for classroom instruction and learning. One of the limitations of this method is that it is not sensitive to the impact of a few students with a high number of suspensions or of students who have been suspended for a large number of days. Therefore, after using this method, we recommend that you review the individual patterns of students suspended at your school to determine whether this is a factor.

Suspension data may also be a reflection of educators' differential responses to student behavior. There are data that indicate a cultural bias to student suspensions that may be grounded in cultural differences between educators and students (Bay Area School Reform Collaborative, 2001).

Information required for this comparison is the total number of students in each demographic group at your school and the total number of days students were suspended for each demographic group being compared. This information allows you to calculate the average number of days each student was suspended for each demographic group. The establishment of a criterion to determine whether there are educationally significant differences between demographic groups for suspensions is more difficult than some of the other measures because of the low incidence of suspensions. We suggest that when one demographic group's suspension rate is twice as high or higher than that of any other demographic group, the averages be considered an educationally significant difference. For example, if the average number of days of suspension for one demographic group is 0.25, then the other group average must equal or exceed 0.50 to demonstrate an educationally significant difference between the two groups. As with prior illustrations, adjust this criterion if it seems more appropriate to do so in your school setting.

■ ABC School Case Study for Suspension Data

Students and educators in the ABC Case Study Elementary School lost 203 instructional days to suspensions during the school year. Table 8.3 provides an analysis of the number of days of suspension for demographic group comparisons. Operational definitions for the column headings are

1. *Demographic Groups*—the demographic groups being studied.

2. *Number of Students*—the number of students in each demographic group comparison. Remember to consider data for

English language learning students separately and not within any other demographic group. Also, a demographic group has to include at least 30 students to yield reliable data.

3. *Total Days Suspended*—the total number of days students were suspended per demographic student group.

4. *Average Number of Days Suspended*—the average number of days each demographic group was suspended. The average is computed by dividing the total days of suspension (column 3) by the number of students (column 2). For example, for the African American demographic group average, dividing the number of days suspended (i.e., 76) by the number of African American students (i.e., 107) yields an average of 0.71 days per student. For their peer group, you divide 94 by 442 and derive an average of 0.21 days per student.

5. *Rate of Suspensions Between Groups*—the rate of the differences between the average suspensions between the two values. This figure represents the rate of the difference between the two groups' average scores. For example, the rate for the African American demographic group and the peer demographic group is 3.4, indicating that the African American group had 3.4 times more suspensions than their peer group (0.71 divided by 0.21).

6. *Significant?*—used to determine whether there is an educationally significant difference between the demographic groups. A rate of two times or more between the average suspensions of the two groups would represent an educationally significant difference. If the difference is less than two times the rate then there is no educationally significant difference between the demographic groups.

Conclusion

Educationally significant differences were found for three of the six comparisons. These findings indicated that African American students were suspended 3.4 times more frequently than their peer group, male students were suspended 9.3 times more often than female students, and the Latino peer group was suspended 4.5 times more often than was the Latino student group. Therefore, educationally significant differences in suspensions by demographic groups were the following:

Table 8.3   Analysis of Demographic Group Suspension Data, ABC Case Study School

Group (1)	Number of Students (2)	Total Days Suspended (3)	Average Number of Days Suspended (4)	Rate of Suspensions Between Groups (5)	Significant (≥ Twice the Rate)? (6)
African American Peer Group	107 442	76 94	0.71 0.21	3.4	Yes
Latino Peer Group	104 445	8 162	0.08 0.36	4.5	Yes
White Peer Group	296 253	80 90	0.27 0.36	1.3	No
Males Females	275 274	153 17	0.56 0.06	9.3	Yes
Poverty Peer Group	257 292	100 70	0.39 0.24	1.6	No
English Learners Peer Group	158 549	28 170	0.18 0.31	1.7	No

- Male and African American students had higher rates of suspensions than their peer groups,
- Latino students had significantly *fewer* days than their peer group students, and
- Male students had the highest rate of suspensions compared to their peer group in that they experienced suspensions 9.3 times more often than did female students.

Your Turn: Entering Student Suspension Data

Table 8.4 is available to assist you in determining the suspension rates of the demographic groups at your school. Operational definitions for the six columns in Table 8.4 are described preceding Table 8.1. If you use the CD, you need to provide information only for the second and third columns. The CD computation file is located under the Data Computation Files as Chapter 8—Table 8.4. The software will compute the remaining table information for you. If you don't have access to a computer, then use the descriptions for each column to compute your values. If you need to compute the remaining three columns, please refer to the definitions that precede Table 8.4. If you are completing your calculations without the use of the CD, then use the blank form on the CD under the Data Collection and Entry files referred to as Chapter 8—8.4.

■ Student-Focused Dialogue Using Suspension Data

Some questions to explore when examining your school's suspension data are as follows:

Are there educationally significant differences between any of your demographic groups? If so, what groups are identified as having a suspension gap?

_____

_____

_____

_____

Table 8.4   Analysis of Demographic Group Suspension Data, _____ School

Group (1)	Number of Students (2)	Total Days Suspended (3)	Average Number of Days a Student Was Suspended (4)	Rate of Suspensions Between Groups (5)	Significant (≥ Twice the Rate)? (6)
African American Peer Group					
Total					
Latino Peer Group					
Total					
White Peer Group					
Total					
Males					
Females					
Total					
Poverty Peer Group					
Total					
English Learners Peer Group					
Total					

What is the extent of the differences? Do they vary by demographic groups?

_____

_____

_____

_____

What conclusions do you draw from the data?

_____

_____

_____

_____

Access Data: Student Identification for Special Programs

Student identification for special education programs in your school is another important source of demographic data. For the ABC Case Study School we identify two special needs populations, students with disabilities and gifted and talented students. Analysis and interpretation of participation in these two programs may pose these challenges for you:

- There may be a small number of students identified for these two programs, which will make generalizations extremely difficult.
- Sometimes these programs include students from other school sites in your district.

If you have the issue of small sample sizes, be extremely cautious in making generalizations from the information. The best approach is to see whether the demographic patterns of program identification are similar to the patterns identified in the academic findings in achievement data set and the other access data. Examine trends among and within these data sets and reflect on their implications for special needs students. Multiple years of data will ensure confidence in trends that you identify. Sample sizes substantially smaller than 30 students can be used as *reflective information* in your overall assessment of student access but are of limited use for purposes of making valid comparisons.

One of the unique characteristics of school programs serving special needs populations is that, for a variety of reasons, they may draw students from an attendance boundary different from that for the general student population. When this is the case, programs that involve students from other schools may not represent the demographic profile of your school. In such cases it may be important to note when special needs programs at your school involve students from one or more cultural groups in substantially larger proportions than are represented in your traditional school population.

Again, because of the low incidence of students in some special needs programs, we established the criterion used to identify an educationally significant difference between demographic groups as having at least twice the difference of percent of students involved in special needs programs.

■ ABC Case Study School for Special Program Identification

Data for the ABC Case Study School inquiry include students in grades 2–6. This analysis, like the others, uses the peer group model and, therefore, considers the needs of English learners independent of English-proficient students. This resulted in 278 out of a possible 374 students being identified as English proficient. Table 7.2 in Chapter 7 provided a summary of English learners by primary language. Adequate sample sizes are available for African American (48), Latino (55), and white (149) students for comparison purposes.

Table 8.5 provides the identification of the 25 students with disabilities by ethnicity and gender for the ABC School. Each demographic group with identified students with disabilities is represented by actual numbers and by percentages. Six students identified as having a disability and being limited English speaking are not included in this analysis. The percentage of students with disabilities was computed by dividing the number of students identified by the total number of students for each comparison group. For example, for the African American student group, 8.3% were identified as students with disabilities. This percentage is computed by dividing the number of students with disabilities by the total number of African American students, or 48 (4 divided by 48 = 8.3%).

Table 8.5   Special Program Identification for Students With Disabilities by Ethnicity and Gender

Ethnicity/Size of Group	Number of Students	Number of Students Identified With Disabilities	Percent of Students With Disabilities	Rate and Significance (≥ Twice the Percent)? (Yes/No)
Ethnicity				
African American	48	4	8.3%	Rate = 1.1
African American Peer Group	230	21	9.1%	No
Latino	55	2	3.6%	Rate = 2.9
Latino Peer Group	223	23	10.3%	Yes
White	149	16	10.7%	Rate = 1.5
White Peer Group	129	9	7.0%	No
Gender				
Males	133	16	12.0%	Rate = 1.9
Females	145	9	6.2%	No

Conclusion

Significant patterns are the underrepresentation of Latino students identified as having disabilities. There were significantly fewer Latino students (3.6%) identified as students with disabilities than their peer group (10.3%). There were no differences between African American students and their peer group, between white students and their peer group, or between male and female students. The difference between male and female students, however, was close to the criterion and, therefore, it may be a good idea for the ABC School to review data for male and female students because of the national trend of greater male enrollment in special education programs.

Table 8.6 provides the identification of gifted and talented students by ethnicity and gender for the ABC School. The percentage of students identified as gifted and talented (i.e., GATE) was computed by dividing the number of students identified by the total number of students for each comparison group. For example, for African American students, one student out of 48, or 2.1% (1 divided by 48), was identified as GATE.

The table includes African American, Latino, and white racial-ethnic demographic groups. This table represents 11 students or 4.0% of the student population. Two students identified as GATE were limited English speaking and are not included in this analysis.

Table 8.6   Special Program Identification for GATE by Ethnicity and Gender

Ethnicity/Size of Group	Number of Students	Number of Students Identified as GATE	Percent of Students Identified as GATE	Rate and Significance (≥ Twice the Percent)? (Yes/No)
Ethnicity				
African American	48	1	2.1%	Rate = 2.0
African American Peer Group	230	10	4.3%	Yes
Latino	55	1	1.8%	Rate = 2.4
Latino Peer Group	223	10	4.3%	Yes
White	149	8	5.4%	Rate = 2.3
White Peer Group	129	3	2.3%	Yes
Gender				
Males	133	7	5.3%	Rate = 1.9
Females	145	4	2.8%	No

Conclusion

Educationally significant patterns were noted for each of the demographic group comparisons except gender. Gender differences, however, closely approached the 2.0 criterion. Students with greater GATE identification were as follows: African American peer group (rate of 2.0), Latino peer group (rate of 2.4), and white group (rate of 2.3). This indicates an educationally significantly smaller proportion of African American and Latino students identified at ABC School as gifted and talented.

Your Turn: Students With Special Program Identification

Tables 8.7 and 8.8 are available to assist you in determining the special program identification rates of groups at your school. If you use the CD you need to provide information only for the first and second columns. The software will compute percentages.

The CD computation file is located under the Data Computation Files as Chapter 8—Table 8.7 and 8.8. If you need to compute the remaining three columns, please refer to the descriptions that are included in the introduction of this section. If you are completing your calculations without the use of the CD, then use the blank form on the CD under the Data Collection and Entry files referred to as Chapter 8—8.7 and 8.8.

■ Student-Focused Dialogue Using Student Identification for Special Programs

Questions to consider when examining your school's identification of students for special programs data are as follows:

Table 8.7   Special Program Identification for Students With Disabilities by Ethnicity and Gender

Ethnicity/Size of Group	Number of Students	Number of Students Identified With Disabilities	Percent of Students With Disabilities	Rate and Significance (≥ Twice the Percent)? (Yes/No)
Ethnicity African American African American Peer Group Latino Latino Peer Group White White Peer Group				
Gender Males Females				

Table 8.8   Special Program Identification for GATE by Ethnicity and Gender

Ethnicity/Size of Group	Number of Students	Number of Students Identified as GATE	Percent of Students Identified as GATE	Rate and Significance (≥ Twice the Percent)? (Yes/No)
Ethnicity African American African American Peer Group Latino Latino Peer Group White White Peer Group				
Gender Males Females				

Are there any educationally significant differences between any of your demographic groups? If so, what groups are identified as being over- or underrepresented?

_____

_____

_____

_____

What is the extent of the differences? Do they vary by demographic groups?

_____

_____

_____

_____

What conclusions do you draw from the data?

_____

_____

_____

_____

Analysis of Your School Data and Conclusions

Table 8.9 provides you with an opportunity to summarize your findings for attendance, suspensions, and identification of students in special programs. Note your findings in this table and be sure to include other access data that you addressed at your school. A blank form of Table 8.9 is provided on the CD under the Data Collection and Entry Forms—Chapter 8—Table 8.9.

Review the information you entered in Table 8.9. Consider both educationally significant differences and the extent of differences. After summarizing your findings in Table 8.9 and drawing conclusions based on the data, reflect on the questions in the section that follows.

■ Student-Focused Dialogue Using the Rubrics and Outcomes From Table 8.9

The questions in this section are derived from the rubrics presented in Chapter 6 and are offered here to help you correlate student outcomes with educational practices you believe to be influencing the student outcomes reflected in your data summary. You may find it informative to refer to each rubric in Chapter 6 as you consider the questions.

At the end of Chapter 9, you will have another opportunity to use your reflective questions for Chapters 7, 8, and 9 to shape your analysis of one or more important subsystems or leverage points in order to prioritize your next steps to better meet the needs of underperforming students.

Table 8.9 School Data Summary

| Groups Compared | Is There a Significant Difference Between These Groups? Indicate With Yes or No | | | | | |
	Attendance	Suspensions	Students With Disabilities	Students Identified as GATE	Other Data	Other Data
African American & Peer Group						
Latino & Peer Group						
White & Peer Group						
Poverty & Nonpoverty						
Male & Female						
Others						

147

Curriculum and Instruction

Using the curriculum and instruction rubric as a framework, examine the summative data for Table 8.9 and consider the following reflective questions. We provide space at the end of this section to record your responses.

- What kinds of experiences are students having in classrooms? Are they engaged in quality opportunities to learn? To what extent are other educators, beyond classroom teachers, aware of and involved in supporting students' progress?
- What kind of curricular options are offered to students? What strategies are used to diagnose students' learning needs, and what data are used to make student placements?
- What is the nature of student-teacher interactions and relationships, especially between teachers and underperforming students?
- How do teachers encourage students to work at high levels, and what kind of support do they offer within and outside of the classroom to help students be successful in the classes into which students are placed?

_____

_____

_____

_____

Assessment and Accountability

Using the assessment and accountability rubric as a framework, examine the summative data for Table 8.9 and consider the following reflective questions. We provide space at the end of this section to record your responses.

- How are students, parents, teachers, and other educators provided feedback about student progress?
- What opportunities do students have to practice their learning and revise their work? How do teachers and other staff collect and use data about students' progress and important gaps between student groups?

- To what extent do educators share information about student progress and strategies to support the learning needs of underserved student groups?

_____

_____

_____

_____

Parent and Community Communication and Outreach

Using the parent and community communication and outreach rubric as a framework, examine the summative data for Table 8.9 and consider the following reflective questions. We provide space at the end of this section to record your responses.

- To what extent do educators seek and use information about students' home cultures to bridge gaps between the way things are done at home and the behavioral and learning expectations of the school?
- How do teachers encourage communication and participation from parents about shared expectations for educational success of their students? How do school personnel communicate the school's expectations to students and parents?
- How do school personnel invite parent and student involvement in positive and welcoming ways?
- How do school personnel share information with students and parents about educational and curricular options?

_____

_____

_____

_____

Professional Development

Using the professional development rubric as a framework, examine the summative data for Table 8.9 and consider the following reflective questions. We provide space at the end of this section to record your responses.

- What opportunities do educators have to discuss the connections between home cultures and attitudes toward school and classroom behavior?
- What opportunities and resources does the school provide for educators to seek and share information and strategies to improve the ongoing attendance and engagement of specific underserved student groups?

_____

_____

_____

_____

9

Data Set #2 (Extended)

Finding Meaning in Access Data Unique to Secondary Schools

There is a growing awareness of the tremendous difference that teachers—and the school climate in general—can make in the lives and future of young people.

—Sonia Nieto (2004, p. 274)

Getting Centered

In Chapter 8 you gathered and analyzed demographic patterns of student access in terms of their attendance, patterns of suspensions, and special needs designations. Now, we invite you to think of your secondary students and additional noncurricular issues that affect their ability to be successful in school. What impact do you believe these noncurricular issues have on your students? How do you think your students would describe those same issues from their vantage points?

_____

_____

_____

_____

High School Access Information

We use the local high school that ABC Case Study School students attend as a sample of student access information unique to secondary schools. This ABC Case Study High School has approximately 900 students. Access information for this high school includes student grade point averages (GPAs), credits earned toward high school graduation, enrollment in Honors and Advanced Placement classes, and student passing rates for 10th graders on the California High School Exit Exam. State high school exit exams have become common throughout the country as a requirement for high school graduation. The authors again strongly encourage the consideration of other access information available to your high school, such as graduation rates, dropout rates, participation in extracurricular programs, participation in student government, and matriculation to college or vocational schools.

■ Grade Point Average

GPA is one academic measure of how students are performing in high school and is highly variable from teacher to teacher and from school to school. Accordingly, this measure should not be considered an absolute value because there typically is a great amount of variation in how grades are assigned within a school or district. GPA is typically computed on a four-point scale. This scale is translated as follows:

4.0—letter grade of A

3.0—letter grade of B

2.0—letter grade of C

1.0—letter grade of D

Below 1.0—letter grade of F

Establishing the criterion of what represents an educationally significant difference between peer groups' GPA is, again, a subjective decision. One-half a grade point or 0.5 difference in average GPA would seem a likely criterion on this four-point scale. This can represent a difference between letter grades (e.g., 2.5 to 3.0, etc.). We use this difference as a criterion in determining whether there are educationally significant differences between groups. You may wish to establish a different criterion for your school or district.

GPAs are computed for the entire school population at this high school and by grade level. Grade-level information may demonstrate different patterns, which might have implications for your school. When looking at grade-level comparisons, one must also consider whether there is any reduction in student enrollment at the upper grades due to student dropouts or other factors.

Table 9.1 illustrates the average GPA for the demographic groups at ABC Case Study High School. These averages are based on all students, grades 9 though 12. Also noted in this table are the differences in GPA between each group and whether or not the difference meets the 0.5 educationally significant criterion.

Table 9.1   Overall GPA by Demographic Group, ABC Case Study High School

Ethnicity	Number of Students	Average Grade Point Average	Difference in GPA Between Groups	Educationally Significant Difference (≥ 0.50)? Yes/No
Ethnicity				
African American	99	2.19	0.35	No
African American Peer Group	612	2.54		
Latino	102	2.36	0.15	No
Latino Peer Group	609	2.51		
White	463	2.56	0.21	No
White Peer Group	248	2.35		
Gender				
Males	375	2.30	0.40	No
Females	336	2.70		
English Learners				
EL Students	200	2.43	0.06	No
EL Peer Group	711	2.49		

Conclusion

Data in Table 9.1 indicate that there are no educationally significant differences between any two demographic groups on grade point average. This suggests similar achievement levels for all groups in coursework at this high school.

Table 9.2 notes average GPA by grade level for the demographic groups at the ABC Case Study High School. Educationally significant differences (0.5 GPA) between the demographic groups are noted with the actual difference between the groups in parentheses. These differences are highlighted to facilitate easy reference.

Conclusion

Data in Table 9.2 indicate educationally significant differences for 11th and 12th grade African American students and their peer

Table 9.2   Mean GPA by Grade Level and Demographic Group, ABC Case Study High School

Group	Grade 9	Grade 10	Grade 11	Grade 12
African American	2.12	2.34	2.06	2.21
African American Peer Group	2.34	2.49	2.60	2.73
Significant ≥ 0.50? Yes/No (Difference between mean GPAs)	No (0.22)	No (0.15)	**Yes (0.54)**	**Yes (0.52)**
Latino	2.19	2.29	2.47	2.61
Latino Peer Group	2.32	2.51	2.54	2.70
Significant? Yes/No (Difference between mean GPAs)	No (0.13)	No (0.22)	No (0.07)	No (0.09)
White	2.37	2.54	2.61	2.73
White Peer Group	2.19	2.36	2.35	2.59
Significant? Yes/No (Difference between mean GPAs)	No (0.18)	No (0.18)	No (0.26)	No (0.14)
Males	2.13	2.24	2.33	2.55
Females	2.54	2.67	2.77	2.83
Significant? Yes/No (Difference between mean GPAs)	No (0.41)	No (0.43)	No (0.44)	No (0.28)
English Learners	2.37	2.37	2.44	2.54
English Learners Peer Group	2.30	2.47	2.53	2.69
Significant? Yes/No (Difference between mean GPAs)	No (0.07)	No (0.10)	No (0.09)	No (0.15)

group but not for the other demographic groups in mean GPAs by grade level.

One limitation of grade point average is that it does not address the rigor of the courses or curriculum in which students are enrolled. For example, the GPA of a student taking college preparation courses would be based on a more rigorous curriculum than that of students not taking these courses. Therefore, you might find it worthwhile to study GPA between demographic groups for more specific courses, such as college requirement courses. Student enrollment by demographic group in specific courses is also a valuable way of determining student access to a more rigorous curriculum.

Your Turn: Student Grade Point Average

Table 9.3 is available to assist you in determining the overall grade point averages of demographic groups at your school. Table 9.4 reflects differences by grade level. If you use the accompanying CD, you need to provide only the number of students and the average GPA information for Table 9.3 and the average GPA by grade level for Table 9.4. The software will provide the rates between the demographic groups for each group and grade level. This software is included under Data Computation Files—Chapter 9—Tables 9.3 and 9.4. A blank form of this table is also available on the CD under Data Collection and Entry Forms—Chapter 9—Tables 9.3 and 9.4.

■ Student-Focused Dialogue Using Student Grade Point Averages

Some questions to explore when examining your students' grade point averages are as follows:

Are there any educationally significant differences between any of your demographic groups? If so, what groups are identified as being over- or underrepresented?

_____

_____

_____

_____

Table 9.3   Overall GPA by Demographic Group

Ethnicity	Number of Students	Average Grade Point Average	Difference in GPA Between Groups	Significant Difference (≥ 0.50)? Yes/No
Ethnicity African American African American Peer Group Latino Latino Peer Group White White Peer Group				
Gender Males Females				
English Learners EL Students EL Peer Group				

What is the extent of the differences? Do they vary by demographic group?

_____

_____

_____

_____

What conclusions do you draw from the data?

_____

_____

_____

_____

Table 9.4   Mean GPA by Grade Level and Demographic Group

Group	Grade 9	Grade 10	Grade 11	Grade 12
African American				
African American Peer Group				
Significant >=.50? Yes/No (Difference between mean GPAs)				
Latino				
Latino Peer Group				
Significant? Yes/No (Difference between mean GPAs)				
White				
White Peer Group				
Significant? Yes/No (Difference between mean GPAs)				
Males				
Females				
Significant? Yes/No (Difference between mean GPAs)				
English Learners				
English Learners Peer Group				
Significant? Yes/No (Difference between mean GPAs)				

■ Credits Earned Toward High School Graduation

Credits students have earned toward high school graduation are a good predictor of whether or not students are on schedule to receive a high school diploma. Determination of credits earned at each high school grade level is based on the graduation requirements at any given high school. At the ABC Case Study High School, students are required to complete 220 credits. Therefore, to be on track for graduation at the end of the school year, freshmen should have earned 55 credits, sophomores 110 credits, juniors 165 credits, and seniors 220 credits. If your high school has a different graduation requirement, then adjust these units accordingly.

We determined the criterion for expected advancement at grades 9, 10, and 11 as being behind in credits by one class (5 credits) as freshmen, two classes (10 credits) as sophomores, and three classes (15 credits) as juniors. Therefore, the criterion for freshmen would be the completion of 50 units, sophomores 100 credits, and juniors 150 credits. Comparisons between demographic groups are measured against this criterion. Educationally significant differences are, therefore, based on whether or not student groups meet these grade level criteria.

Table 9.5 illustrates the average credits earned by grade level for the demographic groups.

Conclusion

Data from Table 9.5 indicate that some student demographic groups are not completing sufficient courses to be on schedule for graduation. At ninth grade, African American, Latino, and male students are lagging behind their peer groups and the established criterion of lacking one course. At 11th grade, African American students are trailing their peer group and the expected criterion of exceeding three course deficits. All other demographic groups are completing the established criterion at all grade levels.

The encouraging news is that in each of the four cases that failed to meet the criterion, the average number of credits missed was very close to the criterion. Program adjustments to respond to these discrepancies should be easy for the faculty and administrators at the ABC Case Study High School to implement.

Table 9.5   Credits Earned by Grade Level and Demographic Group, ABC Case Study High School

Group	Grade 9 ≥50 credits	Grade 10 ≥100 credits	Grade 11 ≥150 credits	Meets Grade Level Criterion?
African American	49.8	112.7	147.5	Below target at grades 9 and 11
African American Peer Group	52.4	110.6	176.2	Meets all targets
Latino	49.2	106.6	176.1	Below target at Grade 9
Latino Peer Group	52.4	111.9	172.2	Meets all targets
White	53.0	111.6	175.6	Meets all targets
White Peer Group	50.2	110.0	166.2	Meets all targets
Males	49.2	104.8	166.7	Below target at Grade 9
Females	55.6	116.4	179.6	Meets all targets
English Learners	53.3	93.6	132.6	Below target at grades 10 and 11
English Learners Peer Group	51.9	110.9	172.6	Meets all targets

Your Turn: Average Credits Earned

Table 9.6 is available to assist you in determining the average credits earned for demographic groups at your school. Because this is a straightforward comparison between the criterion at each grade level and the average credits earned, this can be done without the use of a computation on the CD. You will be recording the average credits earned for each group. A blank form of Table 9.6 is included in the CD under Data Collection and Entry Forms—Chapter 9—Table 9.6.

■ Student-Focused Dialogue Using High School Credits Earned

Questions to consider when examining the average grade-level credits are as follows:

Are there educationally significant differences between and among any of your demographic groups? If so, what groups are identified as being over- or underrepresented?

_____

_____

_____

_____

What is the extent of the differences? Do they vary by demographic group?

_____

_____

_____

_____

Table 9.6   Credits Earned by Grade Level and Demographic Group

Group	Grade 9 ≥50 credits	Grade 10 ≥100 credits	Grade 11 ≥150 credits	Meets Grade Level Criterion?
African American				
African American Peer Group				
Latino				
Latino Peer Group				
White				
White Peer Group				
Males				
Females				
English Learners				
English Learners Peer Group				

What conclusions do you draw from the data?

_____

_____

_____

_____

■ Enrollment in Advanced Classes

Another area of access to high school students is enrollment in advanced courses such as Honors and Advanced Placement courses. These courses play an important role in admission to many colleges and universities. We established the criterion to determine an educationally significant difference between demographic groups to be at least double the percentage of students enrolled in these programs. For example, if one demographic group has 5% of its student population in an Honors class and another demographic group has 10%, then this will be considered educationally significant as the 10% rate is double the 5% rate.

Table 9.7 presents the percentage of students for the demographics groups enrolled in Honors classes and Table 9.8 in Advanced Placement (AP) courses at ABC Case Study High School. In each of these tables the differences in rates between the demographic groups are noted along with whether or not there is an educationally significant difference between the groups (i.e., double or more than the other demographic groups' percentage representation).

Data in Tables 9.7 and 9.8 present patterns that should concern the educators at ABC Case Study High School. English learners are the lone underrepresented demographic group in both Honors and AP classes. The English learner peer group enrollment rate was 27.6 times greater than English learners in Honors classes and 15.4 times greater in the AP classes. All demographic groups demonstrated lower enrollment in AP classes when compared to their peer groups except male students and female students.

Your Turn: Enrollment in Advanced Courses

Tables 9.9 and 9.10 are to assist in reviewing the enrollment of your school's demographic groups in Honors and AP courses. If you enter the percent enrolled for each group on the CD provided (Data Computation Files—Chapter 9—Tables 9.9 and 9.10), it will compute

Table 9.7   Percent of Enrollment by Demographic Group in Honors Courses, ABC Case Study High School

Groups	Percent Enrolled	Difference in Rates of Enrollment	Educationally Significant Difference (≥ Twice the Rate)?
African American	11.1%	1.3 times	No
African American Peer Group	14.2%		
Latino	11.2%	1.3 times	No
Latino Peer Group	14.8%		
White	14.9%	1.3 times	No
White Peer Group	11.7%		
Males	9.9%	1.8 times	No
Females	18.2%		
English Learners	0.5%	27.6 times	Yes
English Learners Peer Group	13.8%		

Table 9.8   Percent of Enrollment by Demographic Group in Advanced Placement Courses, ABC Case Study High School

Groups	Percent Enrolled	Difference in Rates of Enrollment	Educationally Significant Difference (≥ Twice the Rate)?
African American	2.0%	4.4 times	Yes
African American Peer Group	8.7%		
Latino	8.7%	4.4 times	Yes
Latino Peer Group	2.0%		
White	10.4%	3.7 times	Yes
White Peer Group	2.8%		
Males	6.9%	1.2 times	No
Females	8.6%		
English Learners	0.5%	15.4 times	Yes
English Learners Peer Group	7.7%		

your difference in rates of enrollment between the two groups. A blank form for this table is also available on the CD under Data Collection and Data Entry—Chapter 9—Tables 9.9 and 9.10.

Table 9.9   Percent of Enrollment by Demographic Group in Honors Courses

Groups	Percent Enrolled	Difference in Rates of Enrollment	Educationally Significant Difference (≥ Twice the Rate)?
African American			
African American Peer Group			
Latino			
Latino Peer Group			
White			
White Peer Group			
Males			
Females			
English Learners			
English Learners Peer Group			

Table 9.10   Percent of Enrollment by Demographic Group in Advanced Placement Courses

Groups	Percent Enrolled	Difference in Rates of Enrollment	Educationally Significant Difference (≥ Twice the Rate)?
African American			
African American Peer Group			
Latino			
Latino Peer Group			
White			
White Peer Group			
Males			
Females			
English Learners			
English Learners Peer Group			

■ Student-Focused Dialogue Using Enrollment in Advanced Courses

Questions to consider when examining student enrollment in Honors and AP courses are as follows:

Are there any educationally significant differences between any of your demographic groups? If so, what groups are identified as being over- or underrepresented?

_____

_____

_____

_____

What is the extent of the differences? Do they vary by demographic group?

_____

_____

_____

_____

What conclusions do you draw from the data?

_____

_____

_____

_____

■ High School Graduation Exam—10th Grade Results

One of the graduation requirements at ABC Case Study High School is passing the California High School Exit Exam. All students are required to take this exam starting in the 10th grade. It focuses on English language arts and mathematics. Student passing rates at the 10th grade are predictive of their progress in the high school curriculum toward the requirement. We define a difference in passing rates between demographic groups of 20% or more as educationally significant. Again, adjust this criterion if it seems appropriate for your school.

Students at ABC Case Study High School are required to take the exam at the 11th and 12th grades if they do not pass either the English language arts or mathematics test in the 10th grade. The 10th grade results were selected for this analysis because it includes all students and provides data for information for instructional interventions for the 11th and 12th grades.

Data from Table 9.11 indicate the percentage of students by demographic group that passed the exit exam. Passing the exit exam requires receiving a passing grade on both the English language arts and mathematics tests.

Conclusion

Table 9.11 indicates educationally significant differences for African American students and their peer group and for English learners and their peer group in passing the high school exit exam at the 10th grade. Both the African American and English learners demonstrated educationally significantly lower passing rates than their peer groups.

Table 9.11 10th Grade Passing Rates on Exit Exam, ABC Case Study High School

Groups	Percent Passed	Difference in Passing Rates	Educationally Significant Difference (≥ 20%)?
African American	25.0%	37.8%	Yes
African American Peer Group	62.8%		
Latino	62.5%	5.0%	No
Latino Peer Group	57.2%		
White	63.2%	16.1%	No
White Peer Group	47.1%		
Males	53.5%	10.0%	No
Females	63.4%		
English Learners	6.5%	51.5%	Yes
English Learners Peer Group	58.0%		

Your Turn: 10th Grade Passing Rates on the High School Exit Exam

Table 9.12 is available to assist you in reviewing the passing rates on the high school exit exam. If you enter the percent passed for each group on the accompanying CD (Data Computation Files—Chapter 9—Table 9.12), it will compute your difference in passing rates between the groups. Table 9.12 is also available in the Data Collection and Data Entry Forms as Chapter 9—Table 9.12.

■ Student-Focused Dialogue: 10th Grade Passing Rates for the High School Exit Exam

Questions to explore in examining student passing rates on the high school exit exam are as follows:

Table 9.12   10th Grade Passing Rates on Exit Exam

Groups	*Percent Passed*	*Difference in Passing Rates*	*Educationally Significant Difference (≥ 20%)?*
African American			
African American Peer Group			
Latino			
Latino Peer Group			
White			
White Peer Group			
Males			
Females			
English Learners			
English Learners Peer Group			

Are there any educationally significant differences between or among your demographic groups? If so, what groups are identified as being over- or underrepresented?

_____

_____

_____

_____

What is the extent of the differences? Do they vary by demographic group?

_____

_____

_____

_____

What conclusions do you draw from the data?

_____

_____

_____

_____

Using the tables you have completed in this chapter, you are ready to summarize and analyze the student high school access data. You are encouraged to review your academic information (Table 7.20) along with this access information in drawing conclusions about your school's student performance patterns. Table 9.13 provides a format for you to enter your findings for your school's access data set. This table is available on the enclosed CD under Data Collection and Entry Forms—Chapter 9—Table 9.13.

Analysis of Your School Data and Conclusions

Review the information you entered in Table 9.13. What conclusions do you draw regarding the access gap issues at your school?

Table 9.13 School Data Summary

	Was there a significant difference between these groups? Indicate with Yes or No								
	Attendance	Suspensions	Students With Disabilities	Students Identified as GATE	H.S. GPA	H.S. Credits Earned	H.S. Enrollment in Honors	H.S. Enrollment in AP	H.S. Exit Exam
Groups Compared									
African American & Peer Group									
Latino & Peer Group									
White & Peer Group									
Poverty & Nonpoverty									
Male & Female									
Others									

Consider both educationally significant differences and the extent of the difference. After summarizing your findings in Table 9.13, record your conclusions based on the data. Finally, reflect on the questions below.

■ Student-Focused Dialogue Using the Rubrics and Outcomes From Table 9.13

As in Chapters 7 and 8, the questions in this section are derived from the rubrics presented in Chapter 6 and are offered here to help you correlate student outcomes with educational practices you believe to be influencing the student outcomes reflected in your data summary. You may find it informative to refer to each rubric in Chapter 6 as you consider the questions.

Curriculum and Instruction Rubric

Using the curriculum and instruction rubric as a framework, examine the summative data for Table 9.13 and consider the following reflective questions. We provide space at the end of this section to record your responses.

- What kinds of experiences are students having in classrooms? Are they engaged in quality opportunities to learn?
- To what extent are other educators, in addition to the classroom teacher, aware of and involved in supporting students' progress?
- What curricular options are offered to students?
- What strategies are used to diagnose students' learning needs, and what data are used to make student placements?
- How do educators encourage students to work at high levels, and what kind of support do they offer within and outside of the classroom to help students be successful in their classes and make progress toward important educational benchmarks that facilitate course completion, high school graduation, and appropriate postschool opportunities?

_____

_____

_____

_____

Assessment and Accountability Rubric

Using the assessment and accountability rubric as a framework, examine the summative data for Table 9.13 and consider the following reflective questions. We provide space at the end of this section to record your responses.

- Is timely, constructive, and instructive feedback given to students to ensure completion of credits and courses needed for graduation or to make successful transitions to postschool opportunities?
- What opportunities do students have to revise their work and to practice and deepen their knowledge prior to having to demonstrate their learning on high-stakes tests that may have irreversible negative educational consequences?
- How do educators collect and use data about students' progress and important gaps between student groups?
- To what extent do teachers and other educators share information about student progress and strategies to support the learning needs of students identified as underperforming and make important and timely interventions to ensure student progress and completion of work?
- How are students, educators, parents, and community members provided feedback about student progress?

_____

_____

_____

_____

*Parent and Community Communications
and Outreach Rubric*

Using the parent and community communications and outreach rubric as a framework, examine the summative data for Table 9.13 and consider the following reflective questions. We provide space at the end of this section to record your responses.

- To what extent do educators seek and use information about students' home cultures to bridge gaps between the way things are done at home and the behavioral and learning expectations of the school?

- How do educators encourage communication and participation from parents about shared expectations for educational success of their students? Do school personnel invite parent and student involvement in positive and welcoming ways?
- How do school personnel share information with students and parents about educational requirements, curricular options, student progress, and interventions to ensure success in meeting requirements and maximizing postschool opportunities for students?

_____

_____

_____

_____

Professional Development Rubric

Using the professional development rubric as a framework, examine the summative data for Table 9.13 and consider the following reflective questions. We provide space at the end of this section to record your responses.

- What opportunities do educators have to discuss the connections between home cultures and attitudes toward school and classroom behavior?
- What opportunities and resources does the school provide for teachers to seek and share information and strategies to improve the ongoing attendance, engagement, and success of specific student groups identified as underperforming?

_____

_____

_____

_____

Your use of the rubrics in this manner is critical in understanding the nature of the gap at your school and will be central to your inquiry about conversations that occur among adults in your school, which is the topic of the next chapter.

Now you have an opportunity to use your reflective questions for Chapters 7, 8, and 9 to shape your analysis of one or more important subsystems or leverage points in order to prioritize your next steps to better meet the needs of students in a way that moves from identifying students as *underperforming* and identifies them as *underserved.* You may already be well on your way to examining the correlation between your data and some of the conditions that may be influencing the student outcomes reflected in the data from Chapters 7–9.

As you and your colleagues share your responses to the reflective questions at the end of Chapters 7, 8, and 9, look for patterns that emerge. Use the above analysis of the rubrics to locate the preponderance of your responses to the questions with cells on the rubric that seem to describe and summarize your findings. What patterns do you see?

- Do your findings locate to the left side of the rubrics, where descriptions focus on the students being a problem?
- Do your findings locate to the right side of the rubrics, where descriptions focus on educators' practices?
- Does one of the rubrics compel you more than another to target your work?
- Within which rubric do you see the greatest opportunity to begin to transform your system to narrow and close important educational gaps for specific demographic groups?
- How has the process outlined in Chapters 7, 8, and 9 informed you of your next steps? What might your immediate next steps be?

_____

_____

_____

_____

_____

_____

10

Data Set #3

Profiles of Educator Conversations About Your Students

I believe it is a matter of having one's heart and head aligned.

—Angela Louque (2006)

Getting Centered

Think of times in the past two years when you have overheard colleagues describe students at your school. You can hear the comments, can't you? In the space below, record the positive and the negative comments you witnessed. After you list the comments, record your reactions as you read them.

_____

_____

_____

_____

In Chapters 7, 8, and 9, you collected and analyzed data regarding student achievement and access. In this chapter you will collect data that describe the conversations you and your colleagues have about your students. Each member of the cultural proficiency inquiry study team has the opportunity to be meaningfully involved in using the four rubrics from Chapter 6 to assess school members' conversations. Inquiry team members make thoughtful judgments to describe the prevailing tone of conversations about students at your school with regard to curriculum and instruction, assessment and accountability, parent and community communication and outreach, and professional development. The rubrics are used to profile the preponderance of educator conversations and reveal assumptions about students identified as underperforming at your school. Data collected in this chapter are presented in profile formats using the continuum and essential elements.

Educator Conversations Profile

The profile uses each of the intersecting points on the cultural proficiency continuum and the five essential elements of cultural competence of the rubrics (i.e., curriculum and instruction, assessment and accountability, parent and community communication and outreach, and professional development) to graphically illustrate educators' formal and informal conversations about students identified as underperforming in your school. The profiles for each of the five essential elements can be used as standards (i.e., assessing cultural knowledge, valuing diversity, managing the dynamics of difference, adapting to diversity, and institutionalizing cultural knowledge) in developing policies and practices for the competence and proficiency levels of the rubrics.

■ Describing School Conversations

Preparation Phase. We recommend that you assemble the following materials and decisions prior to the inquiry self-study session:

1. Determine who will facilitate the inquiry self-study assessment. The facilitator is responsible for leading a discussion of each rubric by noting the progression of behaviors for each of the five essential elements across the continuum, beginning with cultural destructiveness and continuing to cultural proficiency.

2. Provide a copy of the rubrics for each participant (i.e., curriculum and instruction, assessment and accountability, parent and community communication and outreach, and professional development). The rubrics are presented in Chapter 6 and are in the enclosed CD for you to download and duplicate.

3. Provide small sticky dots for each participant (available at any stationery supply store at minimal cost). Each participant needs five sticky dots for each rubric.

4. Provide four large charts (approximately 24" × 36") representing each of the rubrics. Each of the rubrics is included as Tables 10.1 to 10.4 on the CD that accompanies this book. Post the charts around the room in such a way that team members have access to them.

Each of the rubrics comprises the five rows of essential elements of cultural competence and the six columns of the cultural proficiency continuum. In each of the tables, the heading for the first column is the essential element and the headings for the remaining six columns are the six points of the cultural proficiency continuum. As the facilitator of a professional development session in which your cultural proficiency inquiry team is using the rubrics, you will conduct several activities for gathering data that describe conversations at your school about students identified as underperforming. You will repeat these steps for each of the rubrics until the cultural proficiency inquiry team (hereafter referred to as the inquiry team) has completed each of the four rubrics:

- **Step One**

  o Ask inquiry team members to turn their attention to one of the four rubrics. Have inquiry team members read the behavioral descriptions on the cultural proficiency continuum for each of the essential elements (e.g., assessing cultural knowledge) and decide which point of the continuum (i.e., destructive, incapacity, blindness, precompetence, competence, or proficiency) best describes the prevailing tone of conversations at your school about students identified as underserved or needing to be served differently.

  o Ask inquiry team members not to discuss their decisions with team members in order to preserve the integrity of individual perspectives and experiences.

- **Step Two.** Invite inquiry team members to make judgments for each of the remaining four essential elements (i.e., valuing diversity, managing the dynamics of difference, adapting to diversity, and institutionalizing cultural knowledge).
- **Step Three.** Using the template for Table 10.1 posted in the room, have inquiry team members place their sticky dots on the chart titled "Tabulations for the Curriculum and Instruction Rubric."
- **Step Four.** Repeat steps 1–3 for Table 10.2, "Tabulations for the Assessment and Accountability Rubric."
- **Step Five.** Repeat steps 1–3 for Table 10.3, "Tabulations for the Parent and Communication and Outreach Rubric."
- **Step Six.** Repeat steps 1–3 for Table 10.4, "Tabulations for the Professional Development Rubric."

You now have profiles of your inquiry team members' judgments about conversations at the school regarding students in the context of each of the four rubrics. In having inquiry team members affix their sticky dots to each of the four rubrics, you have a common visual for all team members. Also, you can easily enter these tabulations into the CD included with this book and develop reproducible print profiles of the rubrics. This information provides the foundation for a dialogue about perceptions and assumptions relative to your students, their families, and their communities.

Collecting and Analyzing Inquiry Data

The large charts posted around the room representing Tables 10.1–10.4 facilitate recording participants' ratings prior to entering the information into the CD program. You will note that there is one rubric for each of the leverage points: curriculum and instruction, assessment and accountability, parent and community communication and outreach, and professional development. For the analysis, count the number of participants' responses, represented by the sticky dots, for each cell on the rubric. The CD included with this book allows you to enter your inquiry results and produce reports automatically. As noted above, these tabulations can be entered into the Computation Files directory under Chapter 10—Tables 10.1 to 10.4.

Table 10.1   Tabulations for the Curriculum and Instruction Rubric

Essential Element	Record the number of responses in each column					
	Destructiveness	Incapacity	Blindness	Precompetence	Competence	Proficiency
Assessing						
Valuing						
Managing						
Adapting						
Institutionalizing						

Table 10.2   Tabulations for the Assessment and Accountability Rubric

Essential Element	Record the number of responses in each column					
	Destructiveness	Incapacity	Blindness	Precompetence	Competence	Proficiency
Assessing						
Valuing						
Managing						
Adapting						
Institutionalizing						

Table 10.3 Tabulations for the Parent and Community Communication and Outreach Rubric

Essential Element	Record the number of responses in each column					
	Destructiveness	Incapacity	Blindness	Precompetence	Competence	Proficiency
Assessing						
Valuing						
Managing						
Adapting						
Institutionalizing						

Table 10.4 Tabulations for the Professional Development Rubric

Essential Element	Record the number of responses in each column					
	Destructiveness	Incapacity	Blindness	Precompetence	Competence	Proficiency
Assessing						
Valuing						
Managing						
Adapting						
Institutionalizing						

■ ABC Case Study School's Educator Conversations Profile

Table 10.5 is an example of Table 10.3 in graphic form completed by participants from the ABC Case Study School using the parent and community communication and outreach rubric. This same graphic is available on the accompanying CD for you to enter your school's tabulations and have results to share visually with your staff. It is located on Computation Files for each of the rubrics as Chapter 10—Tables 10.5a to 10.5d.

Table 10.5   Report of the Parents and Community Communication and Outreach Rubric, ABC Case Study School (n = 28 Inquiry Team Members' Responses)

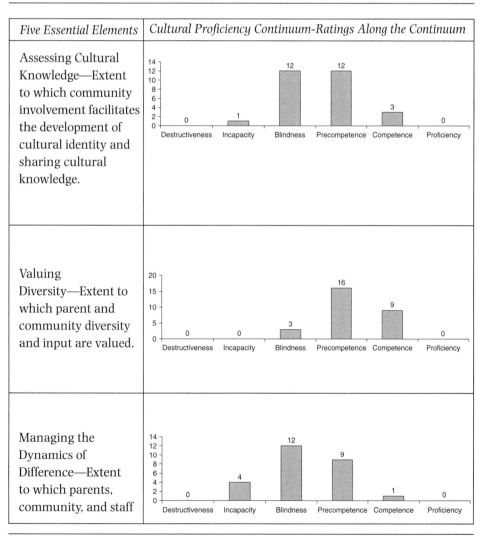

Five Essential Elements	*Cultural Proficiency Continuum-Ratings Along the Continuum*
Assessing Cultural Knowledge—Extent to which community involvement facilitates the development of cultural identity and sharing cultural knowledge.	Destructiveness 0, Incapacity 1, Blindness 12, Precompetence 12, Competence 3, Proficiency 0
Valuing Diversity—Extent to which parent and community diversity and input are valued.	Destructiveness 0, Incapacity 0, Blindness 3, Precompetence 16, Competence 9, Proficiency 0
Managing the Dynamics of Difference—Extent to which parents, community, and staff	Destructiveness 0, Incapacity 4, Blindness 12, Precompetence 9, Competence 1, Proficiency 0

(Continued)

Table 10.5 (Continued)

Five Essential Elements	Cultural Proficiency Continuum-Ratings Along the Continuum
develop capacity to promote and support multiple perspectives and mediate cultural conflict between and among diverse parent and community groups and the school.	
Adapting to Diversity—Extent to which data shape practices, including assessment practices, to meet the needs of diverse cultural groups and close learning and achievement gaps.	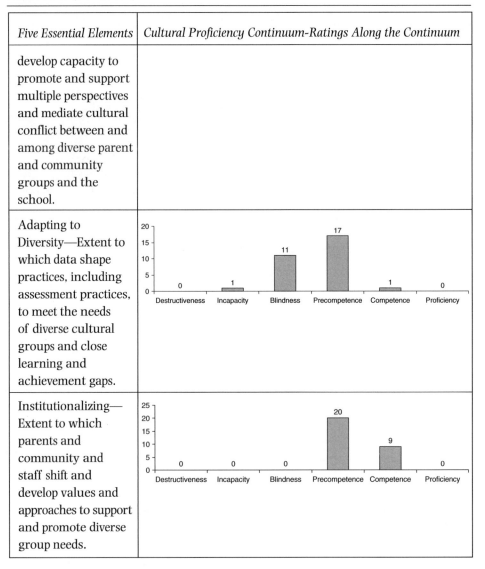
Institutionalizing—Extent to which parents and community and staff shift and develop values and approaches to support and promote diverse group needs.	

■ Interpreting Inquiry Results

The information represented by the frequency tallies in Tables 10.1 to 10.4, and graphed in Tables 10.5a–d, are important steps of the inquiry process in that they provide a glimpse of the manner in which adults discuss students. Like you, the ABC Case Study School collected data for Tables 10.1 to 10.4. Table 10.5, "Report of the Parent and Community Communication and Outreach Rubric, ABC Case Study School," presents two important types of information:

- It illustrates the intersecting points of the cultural proficiency continuum and the five essential elements of cultural competence when considering parent and community communications and outreach. For example, inquiry team members, when describing instances of behaviors associated with valuing diversity, managing the dynamics of difference, and institutionalizing cultural knowledge, identified the predominant practices of educators relative to parent and community communications and outreach to be *precompetent.*

- It illustrates educators' formal and informal conversations about students identified as underperforming in your school. For example, inquiry team members, when describing educators' predominant conversations relative to instances of parent and community communications and outreach, judge the school to be at the *blindness* and *precompetence* points on the continuum, which falls short of the *cultural competence* standard to which we aspire.

■ Locating the ABC School on the Continuum

For purposes of illustration, we are using data from the ABC Case Study School's parent and community communications and outreach rubric. Table 10.6 summarizes inquiry team members' responses to Table 10.3 and identifies the school's current status on the cultural proficiency continuum for each of the essential elements. A blank form of Table 10.6 is provided on the CD under Data Collection and Entry Forms—Chapter 10—Table 10.6 to use for summarizing your inquiry team data.

Table 10.6 Parent and Community Communications and Outreach, ABC Case Study School (n = 28 Inquiry Team Members' Responses)

Essential Skill	Current Status on Continuum	Number of Ratings
Assessing Cultural Knowledge	Blindness and	12
	Precompetence	12
Valuing Diversity	Precompetence	16
Managing the Dynamics of Diversity	Blindness	13
Adapting to Diversity	Precompetence	16
Institutionalizing	Precompetence	20

Table 10.6 indicates that the ABC Case Study School was judged by inquiry team members to be at the *precompetence* level on the continuum when considering three of the essential elements of valuing diversity, adapting to diversity, and institutionalizing cultural knowledge. It is interesting to note, however, when considering the essential elements of assessing cultural knowledge and managing the dynamics of difference, inquiry team members located at the *blindness* level when talking about students identified as underperforming as opposed to underserved or needing to be served differently. The inquiry team will benefit from examining the descriptions in the *cultural competence* column of the parent and community communications and outreach rubric when making plans for continuous improvement in this area.

The numerical count and graphics for each essential element in Tables 10.1–10.4 is a convenient starting point for dialogue. In true dialogic fashion, the intent is not to achieve consensus but to understand the implication of where the predominance of responses place school members on the continuum. When conversations tend to be on the left side of the continuum, the predominant value displayed is one of *tolerance for diversity.* Conversations that predominate on the right side of the continuum reflect a value for the role of educators to be *transformational* in the lives of their students and change practices to meet the needs of students. The intent of dialogue sessions is to promote deeper understanding of the continuum, in particular the five essential elements of cultural competence as they relate to the four rubrics. Your school's profile for each rubric can be used to develop and implement strategies for continuous improvement in order to have school-based policies and practices and educator values and behaviors that

- assess cultural knowledge,
- value diversity,
- manage the dynamics of difference,
- adapt to diversity, and
- institutionalize cultural knowledge.

■ Movement Along the Continuum

Table 10.7 represents the ABC Case Study School relative to the parent and community leverage point and describes the next level for progression along the continuum. For example, Table 10.7 shows the inquiry study team judged educator conversations relative to students identified as underserved about the topics of the essential element,

Table 10.7 Parent and Community Communication and Outreach, Prevalent and Next Competency Level, ABC Case Study School

Essential Element	Current Competency Level	Next Competency Level
Assessing Cultural Knowledge	Blindness Promote and support parent and community and school leaders, agendas, and initiatives without acknowledging the needs of diverse cultural groups.	Precompetence Recognizing the importance of knowing about each other's cultures, parent, community, and school leaders may learn about each other in inauthentic or limited ways.
Valuing Diversity	Precompetence Recognizing need to involve culturally diverse community groups as active participants, staff and other community members solicit input from diverse community members but may not integrate such input into important decisions.	Competency Involve representative parents and community members as partners in making decisions about programs and services that meet the needs of all students.
Managing the Dynamics of Diversity	Blindness Facilitate intergroup conflict using processes that favor majority rule, consensus, or finding common ground, believing such processes to be fair for all but resulting in win-lose outcomes.	Competency Create a culture that encourages multiple perspectives and builds capacity for and practices dialogue between and among all community, parent, and school groups.
Adapting to Diversity	Precompetence Recognizing differences between home and school cultures, parents, community, and staff begin to address needs of diverse community populations, sometimes in limited or inappropriate ways.	Competency Collaborate across stakeholder groups to adapt current practices to meet expressed or implied needs of culturally diverse groups.

(Continued)

Table 10.7 (Continued)

Essential Element	Current Competency Level	Next Competency Level
Institutionalizing Cultural Knowledge	Precompetence Recognizing diverse community needs as they arise, parent, community, and school staff may develop policies, procedures, and structures to respond to diverse needs in limited or inappropriate ways, often containing and isolating the needs of diverse community groups on ad hoc committees or making adaptations on a case-by-case basis rather than integrating changes throughout the system.	Competency Develop policies and practices and create structures that create ongoing opportunities to learn about the needs of all cultural groups.

assessing cultural knowledge, to be at the blindness point of the continuum. A blank form of Table 10.7 is provided on the CD under Data Collection and Entry Forms—Chapter 10 to use for your school data.

Your Turn: Educator Conversations Profile

The rubrics are designed to facilitate understanding of where your school locates on the continuum for each of the four rubrics in order that you may move intentionally in becoming a culturally proficient school. It is important to reemphasize that the five essential elements reside **only** at the cultural competence point of the continuum and that the elements serve as standards for educators to assess their own values and behaviors and for inquiry team members to assess their school's policies and practices. The rubric illustrations for the continuum points cultural destructiveness, cultural incapacity, cultural blindness, and cultural precompetence are descriptive of the values, behaviors, policies, or practices that abide at those points of the continuum that are less than competent. Cultural proficiency, by definition, is a process of advocacy for socially just ends and denotes future and ongoing action informed by the standards inherent in cultural competence.

Once you have identified where you are on the continuum, as our ABC Case Study inquiry colleagues did in Table 10.6, you use the next level on the continuum for a description of behavior that is more responsive to your students, staff, and community. The next level on the continuum, therefore, becomes a discussion topic for how this behavior might look in your educational setting. This level becomes a focal point used to generate short-term and long-term goals for improvement.

In dialogue groups, engage your colleagues in discussing the questions posed below. As you get deeper into the conversation, you may experience group members' willingness and ability to uncover assumptions and beliefs about student demographic groups.

- Where does the inquiry study team locate your school on the continuum relative to each of the four rubrics as represented in your inquiry team members' responses to Tables 10.1–10.4?
  o Curriculum and instruction
  o Assessment and accountability
  o Parent and community communications and outreach
  o Professional development

_____

_____

_____

_____

- In considering the inquiry team findings for each rubric, how might the essential elements serve as standards for educators' values and behaviors and for your school policies and practices?
  o Curriculum and instruction
  o Assessment and accountability
  o Parent and community communications and outreach
  o Professional development

_____

_____

_____

_____

11

Advocacy for Social Justice

Do we have the will to educate all children?

—Asa Hilliard (1991)

We assume that you have a commitment to doing whatever it takes to educate our children and youth. This book is a call to action for those who care about the future of this nation. We invite you, our readers, to join us in taking personal responsibility for unfolding the democracy so that all children and youth will be sheltered within it, and no one will be left outside. This exhortation of education for all students can be traced back more than a century to John Dewey:

> The aim of public education is to enable individuals to continue their education . . . [and] the object and reward of learning is continued capacity for growth. Now this idea cannot be applied to all members of society except where intercourse of man with man is mutual, and except where there is adequate provision of social habits and institutions by means of wide stimulation arising from equitably distributed interests. And this means a democratic society. (Dewey, 2006)

Like Dewey, we believe that without equitable distribution of resources there can be no democracy in education or any other social institution. For we educators to have delayed for over a century to enact this vision is unacceptable. Educating all students to high levels is a *moral imperative* not to be avoided or evaded. In embracing the principle that education is a moral imperative, two questions guide our work:

- With moral defined as "right and just," what will it take for us to get serious about Fullan's (2003) moral imperative to educate all children to high levels?
- With imperative defined as "what is absolutely necessary," what intentional steps to close achievement gaps are we willing to take as educators and community members?

The peer group model, infused with the applied tools of cultural proficiency, is designed to support your intentional efforts to close achievement gaps. Knowledge of historical disparities that are manifested into the achievement gaps identified in Chapters 1 and 3 provides you with a perspective that our schools have not yet functioned in a way to serve all students in an equitable manner. Skills at data analysis arm you with disaggregated student achievement and access data that will help you focus on the educational needs of specific demographic groups. Your commitment to doing what is necessary presents a culturally proficient vision in service of students from all demographic groups.

This chapter is designed for you to reflect on three issues that affect change processes in most schools, and then to have you think more deeply about your data and analyses from Chapters 7–10. Three issues that affect change processes for students historically underserved in our schools are

- *Knowledge*—we have historical data showing that achievement gaps are not new and, in fact, have been overlooked for almost four decades by most of us in education.
- *Will*—our will to educate all children is seriously questioned.
- *Skill*—we know what to do.

Knowledge—We Have the Historical Data

As we presented in Chapters 1 and 3, the achievement gaps have been identified, documented, measured, and reported every two years since

1971 by the NAEP (Perie et al., 2005). School reform efforts have poured from state legislatures and governors' offices for four decades or more. Finally, the No Child Left Behind Act has forced the educational community to be accountable for educating children and youth whose schools receive Title I funds to educate all children to high levels. However, in many schools, including colleges and universities, it is as if achievement gap issues were only recently revealed.

The educational community's surprise and veiled resistance to effective school reform reminds us of Ralph Ellison's 1952 novel *Invisible Man*, in which the main character gesticulates wildly of his poor lot in life only to have mainstream society unable to see, hear, or acknowledge him or his experiences. One can surmise that much of the avoidance of confronting issues of inequity that contribute to achievement gaps is due to the inertia manifest in many levels of governmental and educational establishments. Institutional inertia stems from lack of personal conviction, fear of the unknown, fear of too much work, just plain ignorance, or in the words of Dean Asa Hilliard, lack of the *will* to do what is right.

Do We Have the Will?

For the current generation of educators, Hilliard (1991) raised the moral specter of being intentional in teaching all children in his provocatively titled article, "Do We Have the Will to Educate All Children?" In the years since Hilliard posed his question an entire generation of children has entered kindergarten and has either graduated from high school or become dropouts. What we know is that the achievement gaps of 1991 persist today. National and state reform efforts since 1991 have abounded and, once again, there is renewed focus on student achievement.

Pause for a moment and think back to the rubrics presented in Chapters 6 and 10. The shift in thinking that moves one from the left side of the cultural proficiency continuum, where we tend to blame others for underperformance, to the right side of the continuum, where we focus on our professional practices, is a paradigmatic shift. A major challenge we face as educators is the manner in which we address these conversations among and with colleagues. Advocating for social justice is about *our* moral centeredness to do what is in the best educational interest of our students. Advocating for social justice isn't about what *others* do and don't do. Our commitment to equitable outcomes for our students carries with it the resolve to serve as advocates for those historically underserved in our schools and other institutions.

■ Will—The Educator as Social Justice Advocate

The culturally proficient educator has internalized advocacy as a means of social justice for those historically underserved in our schools and related agencies. If the engine to drive culturally proficient inquiry and close achievement gaps is composed of the knowledge, then the fuel is the sense of advocacy—expressed as the moral imperative, the sense of urgency, or the sense of outrage. This person recognizes that there will be resistance, often hostile, to changing current practice, and he is the one who responds to the challenge by saying "Yes" instead of "How?" or "Why?" Deep inside, the culturally proficient leader knows the answer to "Why?" is having a democracy that includes all people.

The potential conflict between the cultures of our schools and of our diverse communities will be well served by use of cultural proficiency as a model of practice. The equity issues in our society speak to embracing advocacy at the heart of what we do as educators.

The role of social justice advocate is borne of a moral bearing and is not quantifiable in research-based terms (Brigham, Gustashaw, & Brigham, 2004). However, processes such as the peer group model, with its embedded use of the tools of cultural proficiency, equip you with data by which to assess your own and your school's progress in closing achievement gaps. We can no longer add to generations of students being poorly served by our schools and supporting institutions. Advocacy by informed educators passionately devoted to social justice served by a good education is a basic requirement of a democratic society.

Skill—We Know What to Do: Perspectives for Your Data

In this section you have the opportunity to consider your findings from Chapters 7–10 and to develop plans to close achievement gaps in your school. We pose these guidelines for your use:

- The tools of cultural proficiency provide a framework, or perspective, for how an educator views his values and behaviors and his organization's policies and practices. Concomitantly, appropriate use of the tools of cultural proficiency does NOT add to one's professional work or responsibilities.

- The four tools of cultural proficiency are a means to examine your professional practices and their alignment with your values and behaviors.
- The four tools of cultural proficiency are a means to examine the policies and practices in your organization (e.g., classroom, grade level, department, school, school district).
- The rubrics presented in this book are an application of the tools of cultural proficiency to the educational practices of assessment and accountability, curriculum and instruction, parent and community communication and outreach, and professional development.
- As you become skilled in using the tools and rubrics, you will want to develop additional rubrics for your use (e.g., human resources, fiscal resources, etc.).

Transformation for Equity

Movement along the continuum from cultural precompetence to cultural competence and forward to cultural proficiency involves an awareness of one's own efficacy in being able to affect the manner in which students are educated.

An educator who manifests cultural precompetence demonstrates an emerging awareness that current practices do not effectively serve the academic and access needs of all students. It is at this point that she becomes aware of *knowing what she doesn't know.* Educators becoming aware of disparities begin to ask key questions and to decide what information they will need to move forward in a professionally responsible manner. If there is tentativeness at this point in the change process, it is that some feel *blamed* when academic and access disparities are identified and quantified. Moving beyond this level of blame or guilt to commitment to professional and organizational change is a hallmark of readiness to move to cultural competence.

An educator functioning at cultural competence is at the "here and now" stage of the change process. This educator (e.g., teacher, administrator, counselor, aide, custodian, office staff) is experienced as being "in the moment" in performing her professional practice in a manner that honors her students, their parents or guardians, their language, and their community. She is building educational programs with students' cultures as the foundation of their learning and development. Student success, by whatever measures employed, is central to her focus as a professional educator. Student success is her moral imperative.

Cultural proficiency encompasses all that is cultural competence and more. By more, we mean that we have determined that cultural proficiency is demonstrated by educators' commitment to lifelong learning, to social justice, and to advocacy. For this educator:

- Lifelong learning denotes action.
- Advocacy denotes action.
- Social justice denotes action.

Opportunities for Action

Please note that the heading for this section emphasizes action, not planning. Yes, planning is essential to effective action, but too often schools engage in planning that leads nowhere. It is what you do, not what you write or say, that will have constructive impact on your professional practice and, thereby, on your students and their communities.

Opportunities abound in most schools to integrate what you have learned from data collected and analyzed in Chapters 7–10. We need to say again that cultural proficiency is not an additional set of tasks that one does; it is the manner in which one views one's professional practice. Many planning processes in our schools, when used effectively, provide us with the means to examine our professional practices and the impact they have on student learning. It is our intent that you apply new perspectives, insights, and learning from Chapters 7–10 into these current and ongoing planning processes. Typical school-planning processes include the following:

- school improvement plans,
- regional accrediting planning,
- district or school strategic planning, and
- new plans.

Skill—We Know What to Do:
Gleanings From Chapters 7, 8, 9, and 10

From your analyses of the data gathered and analyzed in Chapters 7–9, you have undoubtedly gained a perspective about demographic patterns of achievement, access, and professional conversations at your school. In the spaces below, we invite you to take your thinking to deeper levels of consideration. In combination with the data analysis from Chapters 7–9, your responses to the prompts below will provide important direction for the planning processes described in the previous section.

- What important learning comes from data you gathered and analyzed in Chapter 7?

_____

_____

_____

_____

- What important learning comes from data you gathered and analyzed in Chapter 8?

_____

_____

_____

_____

- What important learning comes from data you gathered and analyzed in Chapter 9?

_____

_____

_____

_____

- What important learning comes from data you gathered and analyzed in Chapter 10?

_____

_____

_____

_____

- How do you see your learning from these chapters providing a unified perspective of practices at your school?

_____

_____

_____

_____

- What suggestions do you have with regard to
  - Assessment and accountability practices at your school?

_____

_____

_____

_____

  - Curriculum and instruction practices at your school?

_____

_____

_____

_____

    o Parent and community communication and outreach practices at your school?

_____

_____

_____

_____

    o Professional development practices at your school?

_____

_____

_____

_____

An Exhortation of Our Responsibility

Our country and our profession are at the beginning stages of a commitment to democracy that is revolutionary. Schools—in particular public schools—are at the center of that revolution that began slowly in 1776 and is now, finally, taking shape in the early part of this century. This revolution is the commitment to all students achieving at high levels. As a profession we are shedding the yoke of low expectations and differential resources based in students' cultural and demographic membership; now we see that it is we who have the power to learn how to teach all children and youth. No, it is not an easy task. No revolution has ever been easy. But it is the right task, for it is grounded in the moral belief that educating all children is the right thing to do.

There are no templates out there. There are few research-based strategies that are easy to replicate and implement. The formula for success is straightforward:

- Adopt a moral position that all children and youth have the capacity to learn at high levels.

- Make it your business to find ways to educate all children and youth to high levels.

It is because of these last two bulleted statements that our occupation is referred to as a "profession." A profession is characterized by requiring extensive education. The extensiveness of our education must begin, not end, with our university degrees. The culturally proficient educator uses his school and community as a veritable laboratory for his own lifelong learning in service of others. It is our journey together as a community of learners.

Randy, Stephanie, Chris, and Cindy, in hopes of continuing this journey with you and to that end, include our e-mail addresses as a means of being connected:

- Randall B. Lindsey—randallblindsey@aol.com
- Stephanie M. Graham—culturalcompetence .stephanie@gmail.com
- R. Chris Westphal, Jr.—rcwestphaljr@msn.com
- Cynthia L. Jew—cjew@clunet.edu

Appendix

The purpose of this appendix is to present a more in-depth, sophisticated, and valid approach to analyzing the achievement gap between groups of students. This approach assumes that the reader has knowledge of statistics and has access to and experience with both statistical and database management software programs. You will also need access to individual student demographics and achievement scores. This analysis is a more valid method to compare group differences because it is based on well-established statistical and research methods. It is the method of preference in establishing the extent of differences between two demographic groups. The text of this book uses a more basic method in addressing the achievement gap to make it more understandable and usable at the school-site level.

What Is the Achievement Gap?

The achievement gap is generally defined in the literature as a *significant difference* between two or more *groups* as measured by an academic achievement test. When we talk about significant differences between groups, we must consider three important factors. The first is the groups being compared, the second is the statistic or descriptor of student achievement, and the third is how we establish whether or not there is a significant difference between the groups.

Identification of Groups

■ Common Practice or Traditional Model

It has been common practice in the literature when comparing ethnic groups to contrast achievement between two distinct ethnic groups. A primary example is the NAEP study, which compares student achievement between white students and African American students and between white students and Latino students. This model essentially establishes the white group as the reference point for the discussion of the achievement gap. It is not common practice in this model to make a distinction within an ethnic group of students whose primary language is not English. This is especially significant for Latino students where, in some schools and districts, there is a large portion of students who are participating in English learner programs. Obviously, inclusion of English learners in the achievement gap analysis will increase the achievement gap for the group in question, the extent depending on the proportion of students in the study. This is true because English learners typically perform significantly below English-speaking students on English-only tests. This difference is especially evident in any English language arts test.

■ The Peer Group Model

Another model for looking at the achievement gap does not establish one ethnic group (white) as the reference point for comparison. Instead, the reference point would be students in the existing system (e.g., school, district, state). For example, if one were comparing African American student achievement at a school or district site, then the achievement of African American students would be compared to all other non-African American students. This approach compares African American student achievement with all their colleagues within the system or their community. Other examples would be comparing Latino students to all other non-Latino students, Asian American students to all other non-Asian American students, and so on.

This approach represents a more valid comparison of student achievement gaps within a school or district context. This context is reflective of local student demographics and incorporates a larger proportion of students in the achievement gap analysis. For example, it is difficult to justify the validity of comparing Latino student achievement to white student achievement when given one or more of the following conditions: (1) the white students are not the students of majority within a school or district setting, (2) the white students are not the group with the highest achievement levels (a common assumption that in many cases is incorrect), and (3) a proportion of Latino students are English learners.

This model also recommends excluding *all* English learners from the achievement gap analysis. As we mentioned earlier, inclusion of English learners with English-proficient students has the effect of increasing the achievement gap between groups when a school has a high proportion of English learners. Instead, we suggest that English learners be analyzed as a separate group and that this analysis also include student progress by primary language groups within the school and district. This approach generally affects Latino, Asian, and white (students from Eastern Europe) populations.

Therefore, the peer group model would make the following achievement gap analysis for a school with ethnic groups of African American, Asian, Latino, and white students. Remember, all English learners would be removed prior to this analysis. Gender and poverty differences should also be included in the achievement gap analysis and, therefore, are included in the list of groups below.

1. White versus all nonwhite students.

2. Latino versus all non-Latino students.

3. African American versus all non-African American students.

4. Asian versus all non-Asian students.

5. Poverty students versus nonpoverty students.

6. Males versus females.

Academic Descriptor/Statistic

Two statistics are typically used to describe group achievement on an academic test: (1) the group mean score and/or (2) the proportion of students scoring at and below a certain performance level (e.g., percent of students *proficient* or percent of students scoring below the 25th percentile) or within performance levels (e.g., the percent of students within quartile or decile bands). These statistics are usually available on reports provided by your district or state.

■ Mean Score

On norm-referenced tests, such as the California Achievement Test (CAT/6) and Stanford Achievement Test (SAT/10), it is possible to compute mean scores on normal curve equivalents (NCEs) or scaled scores (SSs) provided by the publisher. Both NCEs and SSs are based on equal interval scales. NCEs range from 1 to 99 and SSs typically range from 1 to 900. It is important to note that mean scores *cannot be computed on unequal interval scores.* Examples of unequal interval scores are percentile scores, stanines, and grade equivalent scores. When mean percentile scores are reported, they are based on the mean NCE, which is converted to a percentile score by using a conversion table.

Mean scores can also be computed on criterion-referenced tests or standards-based tests. Content standards-based tests are required by NCLB legislation; therefore, it is likely that you will be interpreting student performance on these measures. Content standards-based tests typically feature a student performance level (e.g., advanced, proficient, basic, below basic, and far below basic) and student scaled scores. Mean scores can be derived from these two scores. The mean scaled score for the group is just the average scaled score for that group of students. The ranges of scaled scores vary depending on the publisher and content test. The mean scores for performance level scores are computed by converting the performance levels to a numerical score. The example in Table A-1 shows a typical conversion of student performance levels to a numerical score.

Table A-1 Conversion of Student Performance Levels to Numerical Score

Performance Level	Numerical Score
Advanced	5
Proficient	4
Basic	3
Below Basic	2
Far Below Basic	1

Based on this example, a mean score of 4.5 would indicate a higher performance level than a mean score of 1.5. The 4.5 score would place a group between proficient and advanced and the score of 1.5 between far below basic and below basic. These scores are sometimes difficult to interpret and, therefore, it is common to see the proportional approach that is typically more intuitive for the layperson to understand. The use of the mean score, with a larger scale distribution, is best conducted with scaled scores rather than performance levels!

■ Proportional Scores

The proportional approach is relevant when comparing the performance of two groups on the basis of the proportion that met a certain criterion versus those who did not. This method is typically used with standards-based assessments. It can also be used with norm-referenced tests. An example for standards-based tests would be the percentage of students who passed or failed a high school exit exam or the percentage of students who met or did not meet district or state standards (scored proficient or higher on exam). An example for a norm-referenced test would be the percentage of students who scored above and below the 50th percentile or the percentage that scored within a quartile range. These comparisons, therefore, are a simple comparison between the percentage of students meeting and the percentage of students not meeting the established criteria.

■ Selection of Test Score

The best measurement scale to measure differences between groups is a scale with the most equal point intervals. Therefore, on the same exam, a scaled score range of 1–600 is better able to discriminate student differences than is a performance-level scale of 1–5. For example, a performance level of 4 (proficient) might cover a scaled score range of 350–400 (as is the case on most California content standards tests). When comparing student performance, student scores of 350 and 399 would both be considered proficient. However, one student (with a score of 350) is almost in the lower *basic* range and the other student (score of 399) is almost in the higher *advanced* level. Therefore, the performance-level score does a poor job of reflecting the actual difference between these two students.

With this distinction in mind, the following measures provide the greatest potential to note actual differences between groups of students.

- First choice—use of scaled scores when available.
- Second choice—use of NCE scores. This applies only to norm-referenced tests.

- Third choice—use of performance-level scores.
- Fourth choice—use of dichotomous scores or the percentage of students meeting one criterion (e.g., passing/failing, proficient/ not proficient).

■ Other Academic School Indicators to Measure Performance Gaps

Much of the discussion of the achievement gap has focused on assessment results on norm-referenced or standards-based tests. Standards-based tests typically include federal, state, and district tests. There has also been a more recent interest in student performance on high school exit exams, which are currently required for high school graduation in 20 states. By 2009, 25 states plan on having these exams in place, affecting more than 70% of public school students (Center on Education Policy, 2005).

There are other measures that should be addressed in analyzing the gap between groups. Because these measures are not tests of achievement, the concept of "performance gap" is probably a more appropriate term in describing the variation in student performance in our public schools. The following lists are examples of measures that are related to student achievement and success in our educational programs. The lists include behavioral and educational access indicators. An in-depth review of these factors presents a more complete picture of the performance gap by gender and ethnicity at your school or district. You can also use the peer group model we are recommending to analyze a group's differences in performances along these dimensions. Not all of this information is readily available at the school or district level. The list of other school indicators is not intended to be inclusive. There are other indicators you may be addressing at your school and district. Some examples are the following:

Behavior Indicators

1. Student attendance

2. Suspension and expulsion rates

3. Drop-out rates

4. Graduation rates

5. Credits earned at the high school level to determine whether students are on track to graduate

6. Students at the high school level receiving letter grades of D, F, or I

Educational Access Indicators

1. Enrollment and completion of Algebra 1

2. Enrollment in special programs, e.g., special education, gifted and talented, Advanced Placement Classes at the high school level, and Honors classes

3. Enrollment in subject-required courses at the high school level, which are necessary to enroll in public universities such as the University of California and the California State University System

4. Enrollment in academic intervention programs

What Is a Significant Difference Between Groups?

This is a critical question that frequently is not adequately addressed in the literature on the achievement gap. It needs to be addressed because there are always differences between groups due to *testing error*. Tests are not perfect instruments in accurately measuring student achievement. There are generally two types of testing error: (1) technical and (2) environmental.

Technical error is related to test construction and the ability of the test to accurately measure student achievement. Examples of technical errors are related to the number of the items on the test, timed or untimed test, type of questions (e.g., multiple choice, open-ended, etc.), and the quality of the test items. Technical error is often reflected in the reliability of the test or the test's ability to provide a consistent measure of student performance. The standard error of measurement statistic reflects this error by reporting a student's performance within a range or *band* of scores. This reporting range is a more accurate picture of a student's actual test performance. For example, a student may have an NCE score of 50 but with a standard error of 3.0, his actual score could be from 47 to 53 (plus and minus the standard error of measurement to the mean).

Environmental error refers to errors in test scores due to testing conditions. Testing conditions known to influence student performance are the following: student motivation or effort, and variations in test administration including the physical and psychological setting (e.g., room conditions such as overly warm or cold, poor lighting, disposition of test examiner, or extraneous noise).

Having established that testing error affects student or group performance, how can we account for that error in determining whether or not there is a real difference between two groups? There are typically two ways to establish significant differences between groups. Both methods apply statistical tests between the scores of the two groups.

Statistical Significance

One method compares the difference between the mean or proportional scores and determines whether that difference would represent a real difference at a predetermined probability level. This probability level is typically 95 times out of 100 or at the 0.05 level of significance. Examples of statistical tests used for this type of analysis are the *t*-test to compare mean scores and χ^2 (chi-square) to compare proportional scores. Therefore, if group A had a mean score of 45 and group B had a mean score of 60, the difference between these groups might be statistically significant at the 0.05 level. If so, this equates to 95 times out of 100 you would expect to find this difference (15 points) between the two groups.

The statistical significance approach, however, has two limitations. The first is that the larger the sample size (i.e., the number of students in each group), the more likely you are to find statistical significance. This indicates that you might have statistical significance with these mean scores for a large group of students but not for two groups with a smaller sample size. The second flaw is that one can have statistically significant differences between two groups but the actual difference may have no relevance in an educational setting. For example, in a large sample size comparison there may be a significant difference between NCE mean scores of 50 and 52. However, educationally speaking, there is minimal difference between these two mean scores (both are close to the 50th percentile). Therefore, this difference would have no educational significance; all other things equal, decisions about student performance or instructional strategies would be the same. Unfortunately, this method tends to be used more commonly in the literature. The NAEP report, which evaluates the achievement gap between groups, uses this method.

Test of Magnitude of Difference

The second and preferred method is the use of a statistic called "effect size." The effect size is less dependent on sample size and reports the *magnitude* or strength of the difference between the two groups. Effect size can therefore be used with large and small sample sizes with confidence. The computation of the effect size typically takes into consideration the number of students in each group and mean and standard deviation scores of both groups. The effect size results in a value that represents the difference between the groups in standard deviation units between the two mean scores for both groups. Effect sizes can also be computed for other statistics, such as χ^2.

For easier understanding, these standard deviation differences or effect sizes can be converted to the *mean percentile gain score* differences. For example, an effect size or a standard deviation of 1.00 is equivalent to a 34 percentile point difference between the two mean scores. This translates to a 34 percentile point gain of one group over the other. An effect size of 0.50 is equivalent to a 19 percentile point gain score.

Table A-2 below notes some effect size scores, along with this percentile gain conversion. Marzano et al. (2001) provide additional information to those interested in learning more about effect size in the educational setting. Marzano and colleagues used effect sizes to identify best instructional practices from the literature.

Table A-2   Effect Size and Comparable Percentile Scores

Effect Size	*Percentile Gain Difference*
0.00	0
0.10	4
0.20	8
0.25	10
0.30	12
0.40	16
0.50	19
0.65	24
0.80	29
1.00	34
1.50	43
2.00	48

When one uses effect size to determine significant differences between groups, one usually establishes what is an acceptable effect size or percentile gain between the groups prior to their study. This level, once established, determines whether or not there is a significant difference between the groups. Once the effect sizes are computed, one can determine (1) whether there is a significant difference between the groups, and (2) the magnitude of the significant difference.

Guidelines for interpreting effect sizes are provided by Cohen (1988) as follows: effect size of 0.20 is considered small, effect size of 0.50 is considered medium, and effect size of 0.80 is considered large. Boston (2003) cautions that whereas these are accepted rules of thumb, the importance of an effect size magnitude is, in the end, a judgment call. Kotrlik and Williams (2003) also conclude that it is the researcher closest to the data and design of the study who should describe the magnitude of the results on the basis of the study itself and previous research in that area. For educational purposes, the authors are recommending that an effect size of 0.25 or above be considered educationally significant in determining differences between groups. An effect size of 0.25 represents a 10 percentile point difference between the two mean scores. Setting the effect size too high runs the risk of under-identifying students in need of educational support or intervention or in determining the effectiveness of programs. Setting the effect size too low runs the risk of falsely identifying students in need of educational support or identifying effective programs. With low effect sizes the differences noted are more likely due to assessment error than actual student differences!

We want to make a clear distinction between significance due to statistical significance and significance due to the magnitude of the differences. Therefore, we are making this distinction as follows: Statistical significance will refer to the traditional approach of using probability levels to establish differences between groups. Educationally significant differences will be the term we use to indicate differences that meet two criteria: (1) they are statistically significant and (2) they have an effect size of 0.25 or greater.

The CD that accompanies this book includes software to compute effect sizes for mean scores and for proportional data. These are located under the directory Appendices. The information you will need to have available to compute an effect size is as follows:

Comparing Mean Scores

1. Mean scores of two groups
2. Standard deviation scores of two groups
3. Number of students in each group

Comparing Dichotomous Scores—Chi Square

1. Number or percentage of students falling into dichotomous categories
2. Example: Group A: 50 students passed test; 75 students failed test
   Group B: 40% students passed test; 60% students failed test

Closing the Achievement Gap

How do we know when we are closing the achievement gap? We can assume that we are closing the achievement gap when all the following conditions are present over time.

1. Similar achievement levels between the various subgroups in the educational environment. This would be evident by *no* educationally significant differences between subgroup and peer group.

2. Continuous improvement in demographic group performance over time. We do not want to have a similar performance level between groups without an overall improvement in group scores over time. We are looking for improvement in student performance for all groups.

3. Improvement and equity between groups in

   a. Access to educational core program
   b. Success in classroom work, grades, participation, etc.
   c. Access to educational opportunities including passing high school exit exams and postsecondary opportunities

4. Behavioral indicators—e.g., attendance, suspensions, etc.

Identifying the Achievement Gap: A Case Study

The following case study is presented as an example of the application of determining the status of the performance gap at an elementary school. This example presents the same case study provided in the book, but has greater validity and usefulness in your educational setting.

■ Student Demographics

ABC Elementary School is located in a suburban area in California. The school serves students in grades kindergarten through 6. ABC School is a Title I school with 571 students. The student demographics for ABC School are noted in Tables A-3 and A-4. Table A-3 notes student enrollment by student ethnicity, and Table A-4 by gender, poverty level, English learners (EL), and primary languages of the majority of EL students. Poverty level is defined as students who participate in the National School Lunch Program (NSLP). These demographic descriptions are based on the California October 2004 CBEDS count.

Table A-3   Student Enrollment by Ethnicity

Ethnicity	Number of Students	Percent Enrollment
African American	60	10.5%
First Nations People	10	1.8%
Asian	24	4.2%
Filipino	7	1.2%
Latino	159	27.8%
Pacific Islander	7	1.2%
White (Not Hispanic)	304	53.2%

Table A-4   Additional Descriptive Information of ABC Students

Group Characteristics	Number of Students	Percent Enrollment
Gender		
Males	292	52.9%
Females	260	47.1%
NSLP		
English Learners	145	25.4%
Primary Language of EL		
Spanish	113	77.9%
Russian	9	6.2%
Farsi	4	2.8%
Ukrainian	4	2.8%
Students With Disabilities	58	10.2%

As noted from Tables A-3 and A-4, ABC School, like many schools in California, has a diverse student population with three predominant ethnic groups—Latino, African American, and white. ABC is also similar to many schools in California with approximately 25% of the students being English learners and with approximately 10% of the students identified as having learning disabilities. Spanish is the predominant primary language, a pattern similar to the state.

Student Academic Performance on State Standards-Based Assessments

ABC participates in the state annual spring assessment program that measures student performance relative to state content standards. These assessments are administered at grades 2 through 6 in English language arts and mathematics. The performance expectation for students is to score "proficient" or "advanced" on these tests. Students scoring at these levels are considered to be "meeting state standards." California, like many states, has five levels of performance. The remaining three levels are "basic," "below basic," and "far below basic."

Table A-5 indicates the percentage of students at ABC school who are meeting state standards in English language arts and mathematics by gender, ethnicity, ELL, poverty, and presence of disabilities. These percentages include all students tested or grades 2–6.[1]

Table A-5   Percentage of ABC Students Meeting State Standards by Identified Group

Identified Groups	English Language Arts	Mathematics
All Students	34.5%	47.6%
Gender		
Males	36.4%	47.1%
Females	32.7%	48.3%
Ethnicity		
African American	29.8%	38.3%
Latino	23.2%	33.6%
White	42.9%	58.4%
Poverty	29.3%	43.2%
English Learners	11.7%	34.6%
Students With Disabilities	10.3%	17.2%

Graph A-1 illustrates the achievement level differences noted in Table A-5 between these groups in English language arts and mathematics.

---

1. States typically provide student performance levels by grade level. This analysis combines the results of Grades 2–6 into one overall summary of student performance across grade levels. This gives a more complete picture of student achievement for the school and allows for comparisons between subgroups by increasing the number of students in each subgroup.

Graph A-1   Percent of Students by Demographic Group Meeting State Standards

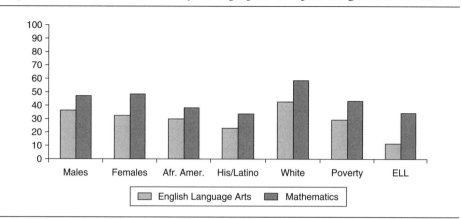

The achievement data are typical of the trends noted for schools with similar demographics in the literature and research. White students outperform all groups, with African American and Latino students falling a distant second or third. Students of poverty also demonstrate lower achievement levels, but this information is more difficult to interpret because it is a group that is not discrete, but instead includes students of all ethnic backgrounds. English learners score below all groups on English language arts tests and similar to Latino students in mathematics.

This type of achievement information is typically available to districts and schools. It is used to identify curriculum strengths and weaknesses not only for the general school population but also for subgroups of students. This type of information has historically provided the foundation for analyzing the achievement gap between various groups. These groups are also included in many state and No Child Left Behind accountability systems.

Achievement Gap Analysis

There are two models of identifying an academic achievement gap between groups. The first model, referred to as the traditional model, applies a statistical test between the groups identified in the data reported above. The second, referred to as the peer group model, redefines student subgroups and applies a criterion level to which the difference between groups has both statistical and educational relevance. We will contrast the two models to illustrate the differences in findings for the ABC School. We will also provide an analysis of student suspension and attendance patterns for ABC School students based on the peer group model.

■ Overview of Achievement Gap Analysis

Traditional Model

When comparing the achievement gap between ethnic groups, the traditional model establishes white student achievement as the reference point in conducting the achievement gap analysis. Therefore, African American, Latino, and other ethnic groups are compared to the achievement of white students. The traditional model incorporates a statistical test based on a probability level that indicates whether a difference between groups would occur 95 times out of 100. If so, then this is considered a statistically significant difference between the groups. Notice that this statistical test indicates only whether there is a difference, is dependent on sample size, and does not define a relevant educational difference in achievement between groups.

Tables A-6 and A-7 note the data resulting from a *t*-test in English language arts and mathematics. Each table notes the number of students in each group, their mean scaled score, and whether or not there is a significant difference between the groups in question. A significant difference in this model represents an achievement gap between the two groups.

Table A-6   Identification of Achievement Gaps Using Traditional Model in English Language Arts

Groups Compared	Number of Students	Mean Scaled Score	Statistically Significant?
White compared to African American Students White African American	161 47	337.1 315.2	Yes
White compared to Latino students White Latino	161 125	337.1 311.9	Yes
Poverty compared to nonpoverty Poverty Nonpoverty	270 96	319.3 344.2	Yes
Males compared to female students Males Females	174 192	323.8 327.6	No

Table A-7   Identification of Achievement Gaps Using Traditional Model in
Mathematics

Groups Compared	Number of Students	Mean Scaled Score	Statistically Significant?
White compared to African American students			
White	161	357.4	Yes
African American	47	326.6	
White compared to Latino students			
White	161	357.4	Yes
Latino	125	325.3	
Poverty compared to nonpoverty			
Poverty	270	334.7	Yes
Nonpoverty	96	366.0	
Males compared to female students			
Males	174	347.2	No
Females	192	339.0	

Based on the traditional achievement gap analysis, ABC School
would have significant achievement gaps as follows:

1. There was a significant achievement gap between white students
   and African American and Latino students in both English language arts and mathematics. White students outperformed
   African American and Latino students on both assessments.

2. There was a significant achievement gap between poverty
   students and nonpoverty students in both English language
   arts and mathematics. Nonpoverty students outperformed
   poverty students on both assessments.

3. There was no significant difference between males and
   females on either the English language arts or mathematics
   assessment.

In summary, the traditional model identified an achievement gap
between white and African American students, between white and
Latino students, and between poverty and nonpoverty students in
both English language arts and mathematics.

Peer Group Model

The peer group model is different from the traditional model in two ways: first, is the reference point for student group comparisons; and second, is the establishment of a criterion for determining if the magnitude of the difference between groups is significant.

Reference Point for Student Comparisons. The reference point for student comparisons involves (1) the exclusion of English learners from the analysis and (2) comparing groups to their peer group instead of another designated ethnic group.

English Learners. Students incorporated into the achievement gap analysis will include only those who are proficient in English. Therefore, English learners (limited or non-English) will be excluded from the analysis. English learners are excluded from this analysis for the following reasons:

1. There is a well-established achievement gap on English tests for non-English speakers and students who are English proficient in English language arts tests. Students are classified as English learners because of a language and English learning gap. When students become proficient in English and academic achievement, they are no longer considered English learners and are reclassified as English proficient. Therefore, including this group with English-proficient students does not accurately reflect how students in various ethnic groups are performing in the core instructional program. Excluding non-English-speaking students places all students on a more level playing field. This achievement gap is apparent at ABC School, with English learners scoring significantly below their peer group (effect size of 0.72 in English language arts and 0.42 in mathematics).

2. There are some significant differences in the learning needs of English learners and English-proficient students. It is important to acknowledge these differences and to avoid grouping these students together when evaluating student achievement.

3. The exclusion of English learners does not negate the need to evaluate the academic achievement progress of these students. There are a variety of assessments available for this type of evaluation. This model addresses only the appropriateness of including these students when evaluating student achievement gaps between groups.

The exclusion of English learners from the achievement gap analysis has the most significant impact on schools with a large number of English learners. The degree to which this exists directly affects the findings of different ethnic groups in the achievement gap analysis. This impact can also be a factor for white students where there is a number of limited-English-speaking Eastern European students.

Comparison to Peer Group

The reference group for comparison will not be white students, but instead the general student body of the school. Therefore, instead of African American students being compared to white students, African American students will be compared to all other non-African American students at ABC School. This acknowledges the demographic makeup of the school and the social context of its learning environment. It also does not establish one group, the white group, as having superior academic performance and therefore setting the standard for student achievement. This approach also allows for a comparison between white student achievement and their peer group at ABC School, a comparison not available with the traditional approach.

Magnitude of the Difference Between Groups. An achievement gap will be identified only if the student achievement meets two conditions. The first condition is there must be a statistically significant difference between the groups (traditional model), and the second is that the difference between the two groups must reach an established magnitude that has some practical educational significance. As we discussed earlier, an effect size of 0.25 or greater will be considered an educationally significant difference. This level establishes at least a 10 percentile point difference between the mean scores of the two groups. Anything less than this 10 percentile point difference will not be considered a meaningful difference (see earlier discussion regarding measurement error). The effect size also establishes the degree of the magnitude between groups, allowing for a comparison of the extent of the achievement gap. The reader may wish to establish a different level of significance that is more rigorous. One should be cautioned, however, that a larger effect size may overlook some relevant educational differences between groups.

Results of Peer Group Achievement Gap

Tables A-8 and A-9 report the findings between the various groups at ABC School. Included in these tables are the groups compared, the number of students, their mean scaled scores on English language arts (Table A-8) and mathematics (Table A-9), the groups' standard deviation score, the effect size, and whether or not there was a significant difference between the groups using the peer group model (effect size of at least 0.25). The information provided in these tables includes the information needed to compute the effect size (number of students, mean score, and standard deviation for each group). Again, this computation is available on the CD included with this book.

Table A-8 Magnitude of Achievement Gap Using Peer Group Comparisons in English Language Arts

Groups Compared	Number Students	Mean Scaled Score	Standard Deviation	Effect Size	Mean Percentile Difference	Significant? (Effect Size ≥ 0.25)
African American compared to Peer Group						
African American	47	315.2	53.67	0.48	18	YES
School Peer Group	224	338.78	48.57			
Latino compared to Peer Group						
Latino	54	331.9	47.04	0.07	3	NO
School Peer Group	217	335.4	51.02			
White compared to Peer Group						
White	144	341.0	48.86	0.27	11	YES
School Peer Group	127	327.6	50.91			
Poverty compared to Nonpoverty Group						
Poverty	181	328.8	49.83	0.35	14	YES
Nonpoverty	90	346.4	49.101			
Males compared to Females						
Males	126	332.6	49.58	0.08	3	NO
Females	145	336.5	50.82			

Table A-9   Magnitude of Achievement Gap Using Peer Group Comparisons in
Mathematics

Groups Compared	Number Students	Mean Scaled Score	Standard Deviation	Effect Size	Mean Percentile Difference	Significant? (Effect Size ≥ 0.25)
African American compared to Peer Group						
African American	47	326.6	78.18	0.42	16	YES
School Peer Group	224	355.0	64.51			
Latino compared to Peer Group						
Latino	54	342.4	70.62	0.14	5	NO
School Peer Group	217	352.0	67.09			
White compared to Peer Group						
White	144	357.9	64.21	0.25	10	YES
School Peer Group	127	341.2	70.83			
Poverty compared to Nonpoverty Group						
Poverty	181	342.8	65.56	0.33	13	YES
Nonpoverty	90	364.7	70.15			
Males compared to Females						
Males	126	355.6	73.09	0.15	6	NO
Females	145	343.3	62.67			

This achievement gap analysis concludes the following:

1. There are no significant differences in Latino student achievement gaps in either English language arts or mathematics
   when compared to their peer group. This is in direct contrast
   to the traditional model where there was a significant gap
   between Latino and white students. The achievement gap
   reported in the traditional model was directly related to the
   inclusion of Latino students who were not English proficient.

2. When reviewing the magnitude of the difference between groups with the effect size, the achievement gap is greatest for African American students. The effect size of 0.42–0.48 was greater than the poverty and nonpoverty group and the white and peer group. These scores indicate that African American students, on the average, score 16–18 percentile points below their peer group at ABC School.

3. The second largest gap was for poverty students. This gap is more difficult to interpret because it is not a discrete group but instead a mixed group of students of different ethnicity and gender. For example, 90% of African American students at ABC participate in the National School Lunch Program.

Student Performance Gaps on Behavior Indicators

We present examples of analyzing performance gaps on behavioral *indicators* for ABC School for suspensions and student attendance. As we noted in the book, there are a variety of behavior or academic indicators that can be used in such an analysis. Again, the question is whether or not there are educationally significant gaps between African American, Latino, white, poverty, and English learning students on these two dimensions. Both student absences and suspensions are directly related to student opportunity to learn.

■ Absences

We defined student absences for this analysis by computing the ratio of student absences during the school year. We computed this ratio by dividing the number of days the student was absent during the school year by the total days the student had been enrolled at ABC School. For example, a student absent for 15 days and enrolled for 180 days would have a ratio of 0.083. Translated, this would indicate that the student was absent for 8.3% of the school year.

For purposes of this analysis, students were included only if they were enrolled more than 50% of the school year, or 91 or more days. This eliminates transient students whose ratio might be different than students enrolled at the ABC School for the majority of the school year. Using this criterion, 546 ABC students were included in this analysis.

The average percentages of days that subgroups were absent for the 2004–2005 school year are noted in Table A-10, which includes each subgroup, along with its comparison peer group. Included in this table are the mean percentage absent, the standard deviation of the mean score, the effect size or magnitude of difference, the mean percentile gain, and whether or not there was an educationally significant difference between the groups using the peer group model (effect size of at least 0.25).

Table A-10 Magnitude of Gap, Comparison to ABC Student Peer Group, Percent of Absences

Groups Compared	Number Students	Mean	Standard Deviation	Effect Size	Mean Percentile Difference	Significant? (Effect Size ≥ 0.25)
Ethnicity						
African American	75	15.7%	.087	0.57	22	YES
Peer Group	339	9.7%	.054			
Latino	85	4.9%	.049	0.23	9	NO
Peer Group	329	6.3%	.063			
White	221	5.5%	.055	0.17	6	NO
Peer Group	193	6.5%	.065			
Gender						
Males	202	6.3%	.063	0.11	4	NO
Females	212	5.7%	.057			
English Learners						
EL	132	7.4%	.041	0.34	13	YES
Peer Group	414	10.8%	.060			
Poverty vs. Nonpoverty						
Poverty	190	7.4%	.075	0.46	18	YES
Peer Group	100	4.4%	.038			

The absence gap analysis for ABC students indicates the following findings related to student absences:

1. There were *no* educationally significant differences in the percentage of days students were absent for the following groups:

   a. Males and females
   b. Latinos and their peer group
   c. Whites and their peer group

2. Educationally significant differences, however, were found for the following groups:

   a. African American students showed significantly more absences when compared to their peer group. The effect size was 0.57, representing approximately a 22 percentile point difference between the average of days absent.

   b. Poverty students showed significantly more absences when compared to their peer group. The effect size was 0.46, representing approximately an 18 percentile point difference between the average of days absent.

   c. English learners showed significantly fewer absences than their peer group. The effect size was 0.34, representing approximately a 13 percentile point difference between the groups.

■ Suspensions

Seventy students were suspended at ABC School during the 2004–2005 school year. Out of these 70 suspensions, 14 students were English learners. Of the remaining 56 English-speaking students, 21 students were African American, 7 Latino, and 25 white. The 70 students also included 34 poverty students and 53 male students.

The suspension data include all students enrolled at ABC School during the 2004–2005 school year, including English learners. This total of 707 students was used to define the two groups being compared, the subgroup in question and their peer group. The total enrollment during the year for English-speaking students was 549. The use of CBEDS data would provide an inaccurate student count because it was only reflective of student enrollment as of one date (October 2004).

The number of suspensions for each group compared for the 2004–2005 school year is noted in Table A-11, which includes each subgroup along with its comparison peer group. This table includes the number of days suspended and not suspended for each group, along with the effect size of the difference between each group comparison, the mean percentile difference, and whether the difference between the groups was significant. Statistical significance and the χ^2 were based on a 2×2 dichotomous table that compared the number of days suspended versus nonsuspended students. This χ^2 statistic is included on the book's CD.

Table A-11   Percentage of Days of Suspensions for Groups

Groups Compared	Number Students	Number Suspended	Number Not Suspended	Effect Size	Mean Percentile Difference	Significant? (Effect Size ≥ 0.25)
Ethnicity						
African American	107	21	86	0.58	22	YES
Peer Group	549	35	407			
Latino	104	7	97	0.30	11	NO*
Peer Group	445	49	396			
White	271	25	271	0.23	9	NO
Peer Group	222	31	222			
Gender						
Males	275	44	231	0.79	28	YES
Females	274	12	262			
English Learners						
EL	158	14	144	0.09	3	NO
Peer Group	549	56	493			
Poverty vs. Nonpoverty						
Poverty	257	34	223	0.35	14	YES
Peer Group	292	22	270			

*This was determined not to be significant because it did not meet the first criterion of significance, i.e., did not meet the 95 out of 100 or 0.05 probability level. Probability levels were 0.19 for the Latino group, 0.14 for the White group, and 0.62 for English language learners.

The suspension gap for ABC School indicates the following significant findings related to student suspensions.

1. There were *no* educationally significant differences in the percentage of suspensions for
   a. English learners and their peer group
   b. White students and their peer group
   c. Latino students and their peer group

2. There were educationally significant differences for the following groups:
   a. Male students showed more educationally significant suspensions than females. The effect size was 0.79, representing approximately a 28 percentile point difference between the average number of suspensions.
   b. African American students showed more educationally significant suspensions when compared to their peer group. The effect

size was 0.58, representing approximately a 22 percentile point difference between the average number of suspensions.

c. Poverty students showed more educationally significant suspensions when compared to their peer group. The effect size was 0.35, representing approximately a 14 percentile point difference between the average number of suspensions.

Summary of Peer Group Performance Gap Findings

The peer group gap analysis indicated significant achievement gaps between three groups at ABC School. These gaps were noted between the following groups in English language arts and mathematics:

- *African American students.* The magnitude of this gap was the greatest for the three groups, with an effect size of 0.46 in English language arts and 0.48 in mathematics. African American students scored an average of approximately 17 percentile points below their peer group.
- *Poverty students.* The magnitude of this gap was the second largest for the three groups, with an effect size of 0.35 in English language arts and 0.33 in mathematics. Poverty students scored an average of approximately 14 percentile points below their peer group.
- *White students.* White students scored above their peer group, with an effect size of 0.27 in English language arts and 0.25 in mathematics. White students scored an average of approximately 10 percentile points above their peer group.

The findings for student absences and suspensions were similar to the academic findings. This was especially true for absences and suspensions, where African American and poverty students had the largest absence rate and suspensions when compared to their respective peer groups. The effect sizes for absences were African American students (0.57) followed by poverty students (0.46), and for suspensions, African American students (0.58) and poverty students (0.35).

Other findings for absences and suspensions were as follows:

- English learners had fewer absences than their peer group, with an effect size of 0.34.
- Males had more suspensions than females, with an effect size of 0.79.

Table A-12 provides a summary profile of the peer group performance gap analysis for ABC School. Included are the four variables used to compare groups.

Table A-12 Summary Table for ABC School

Group vs. Peer Group	Measures Used to Assess Performance Gap			
	CST-ELA	CST-Math	Absences	Suspensions
African American	Below Peer Group	Below Peer Group	Below Peer Group	Below Peer Group
Latino	Same as Peer Group	Same as Peer Group	Same as Peer Group	Same as Peer Group
White	Above Peer Group	Above Peer Group	Same as Peer Group	Same as Peer Group
Males	Same as Females	Same as Females	Same as Females	Below Females
Poverty	Below Peer Group	Below Peer Group	Below Peer Group	Below Peer Group
English Learners	Below Peer Group	Below Peer Group	Above Peer Group	Same as Peer Group

We recommend that the peer group model be used with other school achievement information available to the school site. Also, there are numerous other behavioral or access indicators of the performance gap. Some of these are noted in Chapter 9, "Finding Meaning in Access Data Unique to Secondary Schools."

References

American Psychological Association. (1994). *Publication manual of the American Psychological Association* (4th ed.). Washington, DC: APA.

Argyris, Chris. (1990). *Overcoming organizational defenses: Facilitating organizational defenses.* Englewood Cliffs, NJ: Prentice Hall.

Bay Area School Reform Collaborative. (2001, January). The color of discipline: *Understanding racial disparity in school discipline practices.* Research Brief. San Francisco: Bay Area School Reform Collaborative.

Berliner, David. (2005, August 2). Our impoverished view of educational reform. *Teachers College Record* [Electronic version]. ID Number: 12106. Retrieved August 26, 2005, from http://www.tcrecord.org

Block, Peter. (2001). *The answer to how is yes: Acting on what matters.* San Francisco: Berrett-Koehler.

Boston, Carol. (2003). Effect size and meta-analysis. ERIC Digest. Retrieved July 12, 2005, from http://www.ericdigests.org/2003–04/meta-analysis .html

Bracey, Gerald W. (2000). *Bail me out! Handling difficult data and tough questions about public schools.* Thousand Oaks, CA: Corwin Press.

Brigham, Frederick J., Gustashaw, William E., III, & Brigham, Michelle St. Peter. (2004, May/June). Scientific practice and the tradition of advocacy in special education. *Journal of Learning Disabilities, 37*(3), 200–206.

Carter, Thomas P. (1970). *Mexican American in school: A history of educational neglect.* New York: College Entrance Examination Board.

Cattell, Raymond B. (1979). Are culture fair intelligence tests possible and necessary? *Journal of Research and Development in Education, 12*(2), 3–13.

Center on Education Policy. (2005, June). *How have high school exit exams changed our schools? Some perspectives from Virginia and Maryland.* Washington, DC: Author.

Cohen, James. (1988). *Statistical power analysis for the behavioral science* (2nd ed.). Hillsdale, NJ: Erlbaum.

Cross, Terry, Bazron, Barbara, Dennis, Karl, & Isaacs, Mareasa. (1989). *Toward a culturally competent system of care* (Vol. 1). Washington, DC: Georgetown University Child Development Program, Child and Adolescent Service System Program.

Dewey, John. (2006). *Wisdom quotes: Quotations to inspire and challenge.* Retrieved October 9, 2006, from http://www.wisdomquotes.com/ 001897.html

Douglass, Frederick. (1960). *The narrative of the life of Frederick Douglass: An American slave.* Cambridge, MA: Belknap Press. (Original work published 1845.)

DuFour, Richard, DuFour, Rebecca, Eaker, Robert, & Karhanek, Gayle. (2004). *Whatever it takes: How professional learning communities respond when kids don't learn.* Bloomington, IN: National Educational Service.

DuFour, Richard, Eaker, Robert, & DuFour, Rebecca. (2005). *On common ground: The power of professional learning communities.* Bloomington, IN: National Educational Service.

Education Trust. (2006). *Yes we can: Telling truths and dispelling myths about race and education in America.* Washington, DC: Education Trust. Retrieved September 27, 2006, from http://www2.edtrust.org/EdTrust/Press+Room/Yes+We+Can.htm

Educational Research Service. (2003). *Culture and learning.* ERS What We Know Series. Arlington, VA: Author.

Edwards, Virginia E. (Ed.). (2006, January 5). Quality counts at 10:A decade of standards-based education [Special issue]. *Education Week, 25*(17).

Ellison, Ralph. (1952). *Invisible man.* New York: Random House.

Engelbreit, Mary, & Regan, Patrick (2006). *Mary Engelbreit and the illustrated quote.* Kansas City, MO: Andrews McMeel.

Franklin, John Hope, & Moss, Alfred A., Jr. (1988). *From slavery to freedom: A history of Negro Americans* (6th ed.). New York: McGraw-Hill.

Fullan, Michael. (1993). *Change forces: Probing the depths of educational reform.* London: Falmer.

Fullan, Michael. (1999). *Change forces: The sequel.* Thousand Oaks, CA: Corwin Press.

Fullan, Michael. (2003). *The moral imperative of school leadership.* Thousand Oaks, CA: Corwin Press.

Grissmer, Dave, & Flanagan, Ann. (2001). *The role of federal resources in closing the achievement gaps of minority and disadvantaged students.* Santa Monica, CA: RAND.

Grunwald, Peter & Associates, & Rockman. (2002). *Are we there yet?* Alexandria, VA: National School Board Foundation. Retrieved February 17, 2003, from http://caret.iste.org/index.cfm

Harvard Civil Rights and Advancement Project. (2000). *Opportunities suspended: The devastating consequences of zero tolerance and school discipline project.* Cambridge, MA: Civil Rights Project of Harvard University.

Haycock, Kati. (2001). Closing the achievement gap. *Educational Leadership, 58*(6), 6–11.

Hilliard, Asa. (1991). Do we have the will to educate all children? *Educational Leadership, 40*(1), 31–36.

Hudson, J. Blaine. (1999). Affirmative action and American racism in historical perspective. *The Journal of Negro History, 84*(3), 260–274.

Jencks, Christopher, & Phillips, Meredith (Eds.). (1998). *Black-White test scores.* Washington, DC: Brookings Institution Press.

Johnson, Ruth S. (2002). *Using data to close the achievement gap: How to measure equity in our schools.* Thousand Oaks, CA: Corwin Press.

Johnston, Robert C., & Viadero, Debra. (2000). Unmet promise: Raising minority achievement. *Education Week, 19*(27), 1, 18–21.

Kegan, Robert, & Lahey, Lisa Laskow. (2001). *How the way we talk can change the way we work: Seven languages for transformation.* San Francisco: Jossey Bass.

Knowles, Elizabeth. (2003). Disraeli, Benjamin, in Elizabeth Knowles (Ed.), *The Concise Oxford Dictionary of Quotations* [Electronic version]. Oxford, England: Oxford University Press. Retrieved February 20, 2007, from http://www.oxfordreference.com/views/ENTRY.html?subview=Main& entry=t91.e755

Kohn, Alfie. (1998). Only for my kid: How parents of privilege undermine school reform. *Phi Delta Kappan, 79*(8), 569–577.

Kotrlik, Joe W., & Williams, Heather A. (2003). The incorporation of effect size in information technology, learning, and performance research. *Information Technology, Learning, and Performance Journal, 21*(1). Retrieved July 12, 2005, from http://osra.org/itlpj/kotrlikwilliamsspring 2003.pdf

Kousser, J. Morgan. (1984). Suffrage. In Greene, J.P. (Ed.), *Encyclopedia of American political history: Studies of the principal movements and ideas* (Vol. 1–3, pp. 1236–1258). New York: Scribner.

Kozol, Jonathan. (2005). *The shame of the nation—The restoration of apartheid schooling in America.* New York: Crown.

Lee, Jaekyung. (2002). Racial and ethnic achievement gap trends: Reversing the progress toward equity? *Educational Researcher, 31*(1), 3–12.

Lindsey, Randall B., Nuri Robins, Kikanza, & Terrell, Raymond D. (2003). *Cultural proficiency: A manual for school leaders* (2nd ed.). Thousand Oaks, CA: Corwin Press.

Lindsey, Randall B., Roberts, Laraine M., & CampbellJones, Franklin. (2005). *The culturally proficient school: An implementation guide for school leaders.* Thousand Oaks, CA: Corwin Press.

Louque, Angela. (2006). Personal correspondence, September 6, 2006.

Mann, Horace. (2006). *Brainy Quotes.* Retrieved October 9, 2006, from http://www.brainyquote.com/quotes/authors/h/horace_mann.html

Marzano, Robert J. (1998, December). Rethinking tests and performance tasks. *School Administrator, 55*(11), 10–12.

Marzano, Robert J., Pickering, Debra J., & Pollock, Jane E. (2001). *Classroom instruction that works: Research-based strategies for increasing student achievement.* Alexandria, VA: Association for Supervision and Curriculum Development.

McREL. (2000). *Including at-risk students in standards-based reform: A report on McREL's diversity roundtable II.* Aurora, CO: Mid-continent Research for Education and Learning.

National Center for Education Statistics. (2005). *Digest of education statistics, 2005.* Jessup, MD: American Institutes for Research (CRESS). (ERIC Document Reproduction Services No. ED492945)

Nieto, Sonia. (2004). *Affirming diversity: The sociopolitical context of multicultural education* (5th ed.). New York: Teachers College Press.

Nuri Robins, Kikanza, Lindsey, Randall B., Lindsey, Delores B., & Terrell, Raymond D. (2006). *Culturally proficient instruction: A guide for people who teach* (2nd ed.). Thousand Oaks, CA: Corwin Press.

Ogbu, John U. (1992). Understanding cultural diversity and learning. *Educational Researcher, 21*(8), 5–14.

Ogbu, John U., & Matute-Bianchi, Maria Eugenia. (1990). Understanding sociocultural factors: Knowledge, identity and school adjustment. In

Charles Leyba (Ed.), *Beyond language: Social and cultural factors in schooling language minority students.* Los Angeles: California State University Press.

Pascale, Pietro, & Jakubovic, Shaena. (1971). *The impossible dream: A culture-free test.* (ERIC Document Reproduction Service No. ED054217)

Peck, M. Scott. (2000). *Abounding grace: An anthology of wisdom.* Kansas City, MO: Andrews McMeel.

Perie, Marianne, Moran, Rebecca, & Lutkus, Anthony D. (2005). *NAEP 2004 trends in academic progress: Three decades of student performance in reading and mathematics* (NCES 2005–464). U.S. Department of Education, Institute of Education Sciences, National Center for Education Statistics. Washington, DC: Government Printing Office.

Peske, Heather, & Haycock, Katie. (2006). *Teaching inequality—How poor and minority students are shortchanged on teacher quality.* Washington, DC: The Education Trust.

Picucci, Ali Callicoatte, Brownson, Amanda, Kahlert, Rahel, & Sobel, Andrew. (2002). *Drive to succeed: High performing, high poverty, turn-around middle schools* (Vol. 1). Austin, TX: Charles Dana Center at the University of Texas.

Powers, Jeanne M. (2004). High-stakes accountability and equity: Using evidence from California's Public Schools Accountability Act to address the issues in *Williams v. State of California. American Educational Research Journal, 41*(4), 763–795. Retrieved September 19, 2006, from ABI/INFORM Global database. (Document ID: 809399361.)

Prensky, Marc. (2006). *"Don't bother me Mom, I'm learning!": How computer and video games are preparing your kids for twenty-first century success and how you can help!* St. Paul, MN: Paragon House.

Reeves, Douglas B. (2000). *Accountability in action: A blueprint for learning organizations.* Denver, CO: Center for Performance Assessment.

Reeves, Douglas B. (2006). *The learning leader: How to focus school improvement for better results.* Alexandria, VA: Association for Supervision and Curriculum Development.

Richardson, John G. (1980). Variation in date of enactment of compulsory school attendance laws: An empirical inquiry. *Sociology of Education, 53*(3), 153–163.

Rothstein, Richard. (2004). *Class and schools: Using social, economic and educational reform to close the Black-White achievement gap.* New York: Teachers College Press.

Schein, Edgar. (1989). *Organizational culture and leadership: A dynamic view.* San Francisco: Jossey-Bass.

Senge, Peter, Cambron, Nelda H., McCabe, Timothy Lucas, Kleiner, Art, Dutton, Janis, & Smith, Bryan. (2000). *Schools that learn: A fifth discipline fieldbook for educators, parents, and everyone who cares about education.* New York: Doubleday.

Senge, Peter, Kleiner, Art, Roberts, Charlotte, Roth, George, Ross, Richard B., & Smith, Bryan S. (1999). *The dance of change.* New York: Doubleday.

Sigler, Jay A. (Ed.). (1998). *Civil rights in America: 1500 to the present.* Detroit: Gale Research.

Solomon, Gwen, Allen, Nancy, & Resta, Paul. (2003). *Toward digital equity: Bridging the divide in education.* Boston: Allyn and Bacon.

Starnes, Bobby Ann. (2006). What we don't know can hurt them: White teachers, Indian children. *Phi Delta Kappan, 87*(5), 384–392.

Steele, Claude M., & Aronson, Joshua (1995). Stereotype threat and the intellectual test performance of African-Americans. *Journal of Personality and Social Psychology, 69,* 797–811.

Takaki, Ron. (1993). *A different mirror: A history of multicultural America.* Boston: Little Brown & Co.

Toffler, Alvin. (2006). *Wisdom Quotes: Quotations to Inspire and Challenge.* Retrieved October 9, 2006, from http://www.wisdomquotes.com/001561.html.

Trumbull, Elise (2005). Language and assessment. In Elise Trumbull and Beverly Farr, *Language and Learning: What Teachers Need to Know* (269–297). Norwood, MA: Christopher Gordon.

Unger, Harlow G. (2001). Compulsory education. In *Encyclopedia of American Education* (2nd ed., pp. 275–276). New York: Facts on File.

Viadero, Debra. (2000). Lags in minority achievement defy traditional explanations. *Education Week, 19*(28), 1 & 18–22.

Wartell, Michael A., & Huelskamp, Robert M. (1991, July 18). Testimony of Michael A. Wartell and Robert M. Huelskamp, Sandia National Laboratories, Before Subcommittee on Elementary, Secondary, and Vocational Education, Committee on Education and Labor, U.S. House of Representatives.

Windridge, Charles. (2003). *Tong Sing: The Chinese book of wisdom.* New York: Barnes and Noble.

Zurcher, Raymond. (1998) Issues and tends in culture-fair assessment. *Intervention in School and Clinic, 34*(2), 103–106.

Index

CORWIN PRESS

The Corwin Press logo—a raven striding across an open book—represents the union of courage and learning. Corwin Press is committed to improving education for all learners by publishing books and other professional development resources for those serving the field of PreK–12 education. By providing practical, hands-on materials, Corwin Press continues to carry out the promise of its motto: **"Helping Educators Do Their Work Better."**